ERASMUS
AND HIS TIMES

ERASMUS
AND HIS TIMES

Louis Bouyer
Cong. Orat.

THE NEWMAN PRESS
WESTMINSTER MARYLAND

Nihil obstat : Johannes M. T. Barton, S.T.D., L.S.S.
     Censor deputatus

Imprimatur : D. Morragh Bernard
     Vic. Gen.

Westmonasterii, die 21a Septembris, 1959

This book was originally published by Les Editions du Cerf, Paris, under the title *Autour d'Erasme* and has been translated into English by Francis X. Murphy, C.S.S.R.

© 1959 by The Newman Press

Printed in Great Britain
by S.A.L. Printing Company Limited
Painswick, Glos.

CONTENTS

INTRODUCTION

IT IS AN incontestable fact that the world in which we live is no longer Christian. Yet it seems that the ancient world had become Christian in the Middle Ages. Was it then with the Renaissance that the break was made ?

Many, indeed, consider that the Christians of the sixteenth century were unaware of what was required to christianize the immense fund of experiences and new realities that characterized their epoch, and that was why the new world broke from a Church whose representatives were incapable of emancipating themselves from their own set ways.

This explanation is at once convenient and flattering for Christians today. It should cause no astonishment that many of them consider it all but axiomatic. They contend, in effect, that, were the modern world to pay them proper attention, their intelligent sympathy would quickly conquer it, and that this world remains alienated from the Church solely through the failure of its retrograde elements. Convincing though this thesis may at first sound, it is certain that such a simplification fits in poorly with objective history.

If we study the attitude of the Church in the sixteenth century, what strikes us is the confidence of the papacy in the Renaissance. The persistence of this confidence, despite all that could and should have dissuaded the popes, is what should surprise the historian, much more than any momentary impulse they may have had to disparage or condemn.

So it was that the example set by the very heads of the Church was followed by all those Christian thinkers who strove with a like persistence to accommodate their thought to the new facts and ideas.

7

We often speak of a Christian humanism, but it would be more correct to talk of a humanist Christianity. For Christians were not content to Christianize, after it was established, a humanism which owed nothing to them ; from the very beginning they themselves were the real—and most venturesome—creators of humanism.

Above all, this was the case with Erasmus. Our aim here is to show the real nature of his thought. But it is impossible to understand ' Erasmianism ' without tracing its parentage to those cultured minds who, at the close of the fifteenth century, embraced whole-heartedly the new learning that seemed so promising. From the very start we have to realise that in adopting this attitude, far from putting themselves at variance with mind of the Church, they were simply following an impulse that came from the highest members of the hierarchy.

After a genetic definition of the Renaissance, we will enter on our strictly limited field of inquiry. What development, we will ask, can be seen in the attitude toward the progress of the Renaissance of the most authentic representative of traditional Christian civilisation, the papacy ? The question has the advantage of supplying a subject much better delimited than the corresponding one, namely : what was the development of the Renaissance itself in relation to Christian civilisation ? Besides the consideration of the former will allow for a more general answer to the second question by setting up a series of sign-posts to guide us in the tortuous route ahead.

We shall try, then, to point out several striking attempts at a humanist theology, and thus to indicate the truly Catholic tendency in the very current of the Renaissance, from its origins with Nicholas of

Cusa until its final blossoming in the group of cardinals surrounding Pope Paul III—Contarini, Sadolet and Pole. Erasmus finds a place naturally in this setting.

BOOK I

THE RENAISSANCE AND
THE ATTITUDE OF THE PAPACY TOWARDS
IT [1]

1) In this study, Pastor's *History of the Popes* (English translation, Herder) will furnish the background of our development and will be referred to simply by the author's name. We have also made use of J. Burckhardt's *Civilisation of the Renaissance in Italy*, Imbart de la Tour's *Les Origines de la Reforme* (3rd ed., Melun—Paris, 1944). Jean Guirard, *L'Eglise et les origines de la Renaissance* (Paris, 1902) is particularly valuable on Pope Nicholas V.

CHAPTER I

THE RENAISSANCE

IT WILL BE well to begin with a definition of that
which is to occupy our constant attention in the
course of this volume. What exactly do we mean by
the Renaissance ? We know that the name came
much later than the thing itself.[1] The men of the
fourteenth century spoke of it as of a new golden
age of letters and of art, while those of the sixteenth
considered themselves engaged in a " restoration of
fine writing."[2]

We must mark well the twofold aspect of the movement. It was a literary *and* an artistic revival. But
it was the literary aspect of the movement that
first claimed the interest of its contemporaries.
This is particularly noteworthy in the expression
" The New Learning " applied to it in English ;
but the idea was already current in the explanations
furnished by the Italians for the movement of which
they were the inaugurators. It is particularly noticeable in the letters of Pope Leo X.[3] This fact holds
true for everything which the Renaissance owes to
the labours of its men of learning and its antiquaries;
for what was then reborn was, primarily, the world
of antiquity.

1) See J. Plattard, " Restitution des bonnes lettres " and " Renaissance "
in *Mélanges offerts a M.G Lanson* (1922), pp 128 ff. See also J. Nordstrom,
Moyen Age et Renaissance (Paris : 1933), and A. Renaudet, *Autour d'une
définition de l'humanisme*, in *Bibliothèque d'humanisme et Renaissance,
Travaux*, 1945.

2) The word *renaître* used in this sense, seems to have been first employed
in Amyot's dedication of his *Plutarch's Lives* to Henry II, 1542.

3) cf. for example the Bull *Dum Suavissimos* in *Magn. Bullarium Rom.*
(Luxemburg : 1742), t. I.p.540.

Now the question arises of the change in the meaning given to the word " humanist."[4] Originally it referred to one addicted to the study of humane in contrast to sacred letters. But in the end it came to embrace a whole philosophy in which man himself is the object and the end of his study.

It would be wrong to see in the beginnings of the Renaissance a simple enthusiasm on the part of scholars for newly discovered manuscripts. A completely new approach to the art and manner of living could hardly have resulted from anything so simple. Actually, humanism, in its primitive meaning of a renewed study of the literature of antiquity, was successful only because it provided satisfaction for appetites it had not itself aroused.

With the close of the fourteenth century and the early decades of the fifteenth, there was a gradual release from a chain of catastrophes : the Hundred Years War, the Black Death, the Great Schism, and the Mohammedan invasions. By way of reaction, a desire for good living and enjoyment of the world impatiently came to light. Mediaeval civilization, however, reeling under the blows to which it had recently been subject, found itself exhausted, particularly in the intellectual domain. Its own strength had not been renewed since the twelfth century. Thence arose the incredible passion with which, within a few years, an army of fine minds threw itself upon the newly discovered vestiges of a practically forgotten civilization. So the Renaissance with its two-sided character makes its appearance. It was a spontaneous movement of kindred spirits towards a new civilization, wherein the fullest possible share

4) Consult the *Lexicon* of Meyer under the word *humanität*. The word " humanist " was used toward the end of the sixteenth century. Littré does not allow " humanism " except in his Supplement. For a long time the word was used only in a technical sense.

would be given to the most broadly humane aspects
of life. It was likewise a resurrection of antiquity—
a resurrection with its source in books and archaeology—which acquired great popularity because
at the given moment it was capable of satisfying
previously existing tendencies.

But here an objection arises. The study of the
Middle Ages to which attention has been directed
with renewed sympathy since the nineteenth century,
has destroyed the older prejudice according to which
the Renaissance had truly rediscovered an antiquity
unknown or misunderstood since the end of the
Roman Empire. The fact is that contact with ancient
literature, even in the most unenlightened expanses of
what historians such as Gibbon had referred to as
" the Dark Ages," had never been completely lost.
What is more, as regards a revival of interest, we
have learnt to discern two other " renaissances "
before the Renaissance of the fifteenth and sixteenth
centuries.

The first of these was the Carolingian renaissance
in the ninth century. It has sometimes been regarded
as simply an affair of grammarians and school
masters. But it is becoming more and more apparent
that it was considerably more, particularly on the
philosophic plane, with for example the neoplatonic
translations made by Hilduin and John Scotus
Erigena. The second of these renaissances, that of
the thirteenth century, the heir of the Arabs and all
that they had salvaged from Greece, had produced
what can without exaggeration be called a Christian
classicism. Fundamentally original, be it in the
theology of St. Thomas Aquinas or St. Bonaventure,
or in the style of its French cathedrals, it had also
benefited from many of the most valuable teachings
of antiquity.

Some recent historians would even add a third to these two preliminary renaissances : one in the eleventh to the twelfth century, much more directly dependent on hellenistic influences than the other two, and rich in possibilities, which its immediate followers did not know how to exploit.

Before these facts so long neglected the mind is somewhat bewildered. Was there really such a large part of antiquity waiting to be rediscovered ? But this question really springs from a false analogy. Even if we were to admit that the Middle Ages had preserved, or even slowly recovered, a knowledge of the essentials of antiquity (which is far from true) we would still have to grant that the fifteenth century suddenly produced something radically new in this regard. The crisis, and the irreversible change of direction which it brought about, can be analysed in a few words. Until then, whatever abundance of ancient civilization might still have been extant, it was merely material taken from a broken-down edifice to be made use of in new constructions. But what was now attempted, and to some extent achieved, was a reconstruction of the whole ancient edifice. Or, to put it in another way, it was the resurrection of a living body, of which previously only the severed limbs had been known, a body that had been pillaged for the benefit of the rival that had taken its place.

But, as we have remarked, this renaissance of antiquity was simply the means that circumstances held out to a sudden, violent desire for life. This brings us to a more precise, perhaps even a more accurate, idea of what happened. Until the fifteenth century whatever was available of the intensely human civilization of antiquity had been used in the construction of a new civilization, not only religious and Christian, but even sacral—a civilization of the sanctuary. The Augustinian view of politics, which Mgr. Arguillière[5] so clearly saw to be the root of the mediaeval ideal is, in fact, but one aspect, though a striking one, of a conception implied in all civilization. Augustinianism must here be taken in the strict sense of a philosophy in which even the very notion of nature, of a stable substance, has lost all consistency.[6] In other words, the very idea of a human order—even one subjected to the Christian order, but none the less preserving its own status and stability, even its finality on a secondary plane—was unthinkable. No human enterprise was considered worthy of pursuit except in so far as it offered an immediate means to a religious end. The study of philosphy, for example, was only justified in so far as it was useful for theology. The Latin poets were read, but only on the pretext that their study was a useful preparation for the study of Sacred Scripture. The whole ensemble of the *trivium* and *quadrivium* was embarked upon only as a preparation for theology ; so much so that it was taught only by clerics to other clerics.

The Renaissance of Aristotelianism in the thirteenth century produced a radical break with this viewpoint, but on the level of abstract thought. The prolonged scandal aroused by this introduction of the Aristotle of the Arabs into the Christian system is well known. St. Thomas, by reintroducing a world of firmly constituted substances, though still in strict hierarchical order and totally dependent upon their Creator, at one stroke rendered admissible a relatively autonomous existence for man, his

5) *L'Augustinianisme politique* (Paris : 1934).

6) H. Marrou, *Saint Augustin et la fin de la culture antique*, 2 ed. (Paris : 1949).

B

polity, and the activity proper to both. It was no longer necessary simply to subject them to religion purely as a means to an extrinsic end. Instead a co-ordinated order of secondary causes related to one supreme but not exclusive end came into perspective.

This was to provide justification in principle for a human culture independent of any immediate and practical reference to religion. But as a matter of fact, except for philosophy itself and political science in the highest sense of the term, neither St. Thomas nor any of his first disciples seems to have considered drawing from this principle any of its consequences on the literary, artistic, or scientific plane, and still less in the vast domain of what we today designate as civilization. Moreover, the resurgence of Augustinianism in the fourteenth and fifteenth centuries was almost immediately to destroy the originality of the Thomist synthesis and the completely new possibilities it held for life and thought.

What the men of the thirteenth century had no mind to do, despite their clear understanding of the principles involved, was precisely what the men of the fifteenth and sixteenth centuries attempted, though they were far less aware of the philosophy implied by their action. It is precisely here that we discover, not on an intellectual level but within the frame of daily life, the true character of the Renaissance. It brought in a new taste for human things and for the natural world to which man belongs, it gave rise to an effective, even irresistable, if subconscious, desire to exploit its riches for their own benefit. Philosophy was no longer cultivated simply as an aid to theology, nor literature solely for exegesis, nor art purely for the glory of God. Or rather,

these ends could well remain so long as the Christian
and Catholic aspect of the Renaissance of which
we will see the full import later, was not just illusion;
but would have to allow room for, without absorbing,
other more immediate ends. Philosophy is now
used for what it can contribute to knowledge ;
writing is engaged in for the pleasure of writing ;
painting and sculpture are pursued, and quite simply
life is lived, because the artist loves his art and enjoys
living.

This is not to maintain that such was never really
the case for the thinkers and the artists of the Middle
Ages. But what must be recognized is that they
would never have voluntarily acknowledged it to
be so. They would rather make excuses for themselves. Desirous of justifying their activities, they
were always careful to claim for them an immediate,
almost exclusively religious purpose. We might
say that they wanted to do all that in fact they did,
precisely as Christians, as if it were all a direct
result of their Christianity.

On the other hand, the men of the Renaissance,
the most Christian among them as well, frankly
recognized their right to devote themselves as
Christians, in a Christian manner, to all those
activities which they could exercise simply as men.
It is because these things pertain to our nature
as human beings that they will henceforth be cultivated, and not merely nor even principally in the
interest of religion. This is why the resurrection of
antiquity, otherwise so inexplicable to us, held such
importance for these men. For they found in the
past an example of man's greatest efforts towards
understanding how he could himself exploit his
own world and his own nature.

So we can readily understand how the discovery

of unknown lands by a Vasco da Gama or a Christopher Columbus, and of nature by a Toscanelli or a Galileo or a Copernicus, although apparently so completely disconnected with the return of antiquity, should have led jointly with it to the development of a unique movement. In both cases, man and the world, two complementary aspects of one and the same reality came to be considered no longer so that the beholder could pierce beyond them, as through a stained glass window, but to enjoy it for itself, as he enjoys a Leonardo da Vinci or a Raphael, so firm and full in its composition.

This is strikingly evident already with Petrarch,[7] who, from the sixteenth century, has been the acknowledged originator of the Renaissance. Certainly the first Christian to avow a taste for pagan antiquity, Petrarch is likewise the first modern man of letters— that is, the first who wrote for the mere joy of exercising his talent. This is seen most exclusively in the notion of literary glory which he reintroduced, something completely unknown in the Middle Ages, but so much to the fore with the humanists. Petrarch remained a Christian, it is true. Nor was he content with a Christianity superimposed upon his lay activities. He expressly wanted his faith to dominate his actions as well as his existence.[8]   But far from deducing from this as a mediaeval Christian would have done, that he should efface his personality in his work and promote the divine glory through the work itself, the erection of a literary monument became the great goal of his life. With his *Africa* (so justly forgotten), he hoped to immortalize himself.

7)   See, for example what Erasmus has to say about this in his *Ciceronianus*.
8)   cf. the letter to Giovanni Colonna which Pastor cites at the very start of his *Life of the Popes*. It is to be found in *Francisci Petrarcae epistolae de rebus fam. et variae* ed. Fracassetti (Florence : 1864) lib. VI, cap 2, p.310.

Let us see where he got this idea of glory. He owed it to Cicero, whom among the ancients the Middle Ages had most neglected and it is thanks primarily to Petrarch that this Roman literateur was by contrast to take first place in the rediscovery of antiquity. [9]

There is perhaps no work that better expresses the self-awareness—or, perhaps better, self-satisfaction—at which Greco-Latin man had arrived than that of Cicero. Coming to maturity at the end of a phase of the ancient civilization, Cicero was able to realize the fruits of a cultural maturity on the verge of decadence. In his turn, Petrarch, discoverer of Cicero, proved to be an insatiable propagandist—the first genuinely enthusiastic imitator of the Roman philosopher and politician. In bequeathing him to the Renaissance, Petrarch not only portrayed Cicero as his ideal of an artist and of a man, but also as his first master in philosophy.

It is most necessary to emphasize this at the start of the study on which we are engaged. For the intelligent eclecticism, the ease and lack of profundity met with in the *Tusculan Orations* were to serve as as the basis for the philosophy of the early Renaissance. [10] This manifests its most significant intellectual trait and at the same time its congenital weakness. Later, recourse to Seneca will supply a mere palliative—the sixteenth century never succeeded in achieving a true and coherent philosophy of its own. At best, it only amassed a multitude of moral and psychological observations erected on an unstable foundation of rhetoric.

9) cf. P. de Nolhac, *Pétrarque et l'humanisme* (Paris : 1892), pp. 14 and 205.

10) cf. J. Burckhardt, *Civilization of the Renaissance in Italy* (New York : 1956), who discussed this sentiment as found in the *Codri Urcei Opera* (Venice : 1506) fol. LXV : *Non habet huic similem Graecia Mater*—" Mother Greece does not possess his like."

However this may be, it cannot be denied that from Petrarch onward, the dangers for Christian civilization were plain enough. Would not his enthusiastic acceptance of a relative autonomy for man and his world, and in particular, his cultivation of the independence that characterized the schools of pre-Christian civilization, result in a return to paganism, and that within the very heart of mediaeval civilization and in opposition to it ? It is not necessary to look further than Boccaccio to realize how well-founded are these fears. Not only do his works contain licentious scenes, but his *Decameron* almost literally breathes the wholly pagan notion that pleasure without restraint is the normal purpose of life.

However, despite his many attacks on the Churchmen of his day—and the Middle Ages was well enough used to them—Boccaccio was not opposed to the Church as such. In the end he was converted, and expressed sincere repentance for the immorality of his works.

But in 1431 there appeared a book of capital importance written by the man who was to be the literary inaugurator of the whole neo-Latin Renaissance. This was the *De Voluptate*—" On Pleasure "—of Lorenzo Valla. It takes the form of a dialogue between Leonardo Bruni, defending Stoicism, and Antonio Beccadelli, favouring Epicureanism, against Niccolo Nicci—the man who had restored Greek and Latin letters in Florence— exalting what he calls the " true good," that is to say, christian humanism. Valla offers us an undisguised neo-paganism. Nicci's conclusion in favour of Christianity is evidently a *tour de force*. Valla's thought is expressed through the mouth of Beccadelli. It is a wild and raving apology for a sensual life.

Certain of his outcries—for example, those against christian virginity—give the impression of a madman.

The historical importance of this work, and more particularly the concept of antiquity which it expresses for the first time, has not always been seen in its proper light. It is a completely new concept for the Middle Ages ; and it is at the root of what has come down, almost to our own day, as an objective and scientific interpretation of antiquity. It is to be found again in a discreet and apparently purified form in a text such as the *Prayer on the Acropolis* and in an idea such as that of the Greek miracle. It is the type of thing popularized in the work of Anatole France, the France of the *Corinthian Nuptials*, or of *Thaïs*.

In substance it can be summed up as follows. Pagan antiquity was considered as having achieved goodness and equilibrium by the frank satisfaction of all natural desires which were recognised as basically good, particularly when they were sensual desires. Christianity on the other hand had intervened as a troublesome factor. It had introduced an incurable sadness, pretending to be able to refashion human nature with its asceticism. To such a concept a man like Taine seems to have fully subscribed. But today there is certainly no historian who would accept this without a smile. The pretended mystic sadness of the Middle Ages is no less mythical than the Olympian serenity of the Greek pre-Christian fifth century, and both belong not to science but to the imagination. Of this modern legend, which we now see dying, Valla was creator.

CHAPTER II

HONEYMOON AND FIRST MISGIVINGS

AT THIS POINT we may enquire into the attitude of the papacy to these first beginnings of the Renaissance. The Middle Ages had set or, better perhaps, recognized the papacy as the keystone of its civilization. What was the first reaction of the Roman See ? Quite frankly, we must acknowledge it to be absolutely disconcerting. It is the exact contrary of the accepted modern idea of an inevitable opposition between Christianity and the revival of antiquity. The first reaction of the popes of the fifteenth and sixteenth century to what might have appeared—and should have appeared according to our present ideas—a major danger for Christian civilization, was unbelievably favourable. It was not just a sudden impulse of unreflecting confidence, but persistent and tenacious encouragement.

Petrarch had enjoyed the protection of Popes Clement VI and Gregory XI. But there was nothing particularly characteristic in this. It was in keeping with the traditional policy of the mediaeval papacy to support studious activities by giving patronage to those who dedicated themselves to such pursuits. It would have required a singularly perspicacious observer to have foreseen then the importance for the future of the revolution but faintly suggested by Petrarch.

The movement, however, began to take shape in the first half of the fifteenth century. And already, when it was still practically confined to Tuscany, at Florence a Giovanni Dominici vigorously denounced

the pagan tendency he saw flourishing there ; and
this in face of its pioneers, all thoroughly Christian
men such as Alberti or Collucio Salutati. [1] Nevertheless, it was at this very moment, with the Great
Schism barely over, that Martin V and then Eugene
IV summoned the Renaissance to Rome and began
to foster it there. The most prominent cardinals
of the fifteenth century became its patrons, not only
the Italians such as Albergati, Cesarini, Capranica,
but even a German, Nicholas of Cusa, who for a
time served as vicar of the Holy See.

Under Eugene IV and in keeping with his wishes,
Ferrara and then Florence—that is the cradle of
both humanism and the artistic Renaissance—became
the scene of an event whose importance it is difficult
to exaggerate : the council for the reunion of the
Greek and Latin Churches. A better time, a place
better prepared for the staging of such an event is
hardly conceivable. To crown this astonishing
display of Florentine intelligence and beauty, of
which Cosimo de' Medici made himself the first
Mæcenas, the Byzantine Emperor and the Patriarch,
like the Magi of old with their gifts [2], brought with
them to the West the art that had been forgotten,
and the thought of ancient Greece that had been
lost. Attracted to the council in the train of Paleologus, or perhaps fleeing the menacing pressure
of the Turks, the dying humanism of Byzantium
flowed over into the rising humanism of Italy.
From half-starved translators, whose learning was
often of the slightest, such as Teromi of Sparta or

1) cf. Morçay, *Le Renaissance* (Paris),   vol. I, pp. 12 ff.

2) It is well known that the fresco of the Three Kings by Ghirlandaio in
the Pitti palace seems to have been directly inspired by the Byzantine Court
apparel. It should be noted in passing that we do not believe, as do so many,
that the council brought about this hellenistic movement. But it did give it,
as we would say today, maximal publicity, greatly magnifying its success.

George of Trebizond, to the great masters of literature such as the Lascari, a swarm of orientals invade
Tuscany, bringing their priceless manuscripts with
them.

This new source of ancient antiquity was hardly
tapped when the same phenomenon was to be
observed with Latin antiquity. Paganism was revived
along with its culture—Gemistius Plethon bringing
to mind the strange image not, as he himself thought,
of Plato but rather of Porphyry, and even of Iam-
blichus. In a transparent disguise, a neo-Platonic
theosophy came to life again, enmeshed in a theurgic
mysticism that was profoundly anti-Christian ; an
artificial resurrection not only of certain pagan
ideas and sentiments as was the case with Valla,
but of the whole pattern of hellenistic philosophy.
Yet side by side with Plethon there is the attractive
figure of his student Bessarion. As archbishop of
Nicea he acceded to the union of the Churches
without ever going back on it. He became a cardinal
of the Roman church, and a Christian protagonist
of Plato and his chief propagandist in the west.
Somewhat later, but still at Florence, there appeared
under the patronage of Lorenzo the Magnificent
the platonic academy of Marsiglio Ficino. The latter,
who burned a votive candle before the bust of Plato
as if it were a sacred image, could still oppose, in
the name of a Christian platonism, the openly
anti-religious philosophy of Pomponazzi, and the
schools of Padua which ranged from Hermetism
to neo-Aristotelianism.

Here is to be found the origin of the two currents of
philosophy that were born of the Renaissance and
that have come down to our own days. On the one
hand there was an idealism which made itself the
ally of Christianity, although often, in fact, a

dangerous one. It reached England first with Grocyn and Linacre, and later inspired Pole, St. Thomas More, the metaphysical poets of the seventeenth century, and the Cambridge Platonists. [3] Through Henry More's occultism it continued in the immaterialism of Berkeley. In France it was brought in by Lefèvre of Étaples ; and Cartesianism derives from it, particularly in the form propounded by Malebranche and Leibniz. On the other hand, the naturalism of Pomponazzi was to have its own progeny through a Vico or a Campanella, in Gassendi and the French " libertines " finally begetting the encylopædist philosophy of the eighteenth century and all its consequences. [4]

Eugene IV died on February 23, 1447. In his successor the Renaissance, now in possession of all its treasures, was to find on the pontifical throne not simply a protector but one of its outstanding representatives. At this time, moreover, all those elements so momentous for the later development of Christian civilization were fully apparent in the Renaissance, and already merited for it the most vigorous denunciations. Nevertheless, without the least hesitation, Nicholas V calmly placed himself at the head of the movement. [5] He proposed nothing less, in the words of Pastor, than " to make of Rome, already the capital of Christianity, the eternal capital of classic literature, and the centre of art and science." [6]

Thomas Parentuccelli, son of a poor doctor from the Ligurian coast, had managed at great cost to

3) cf. R. W. Inge, *The Platonic Tradition in English Religious Thought*.

4) cf. R. Pintard, *Le libertinage érudit dans la première moitié du XVIIe siècle* (Paris : 1943).

5) For all this, see J. Guiraud, *L'Eglise et les origines de la Renaissance* (Paris : 1902).

6) Pastor, *History of the Popes* (St. Louis : 1952).

pursue his studies to completion. Then he was taken into service by Nicholas Albergati, after spending some time as a teacher in Florence. When his patron became a cardinal he found himself associated with the highest literary circles in Rome. Having distinguished himself in the negotiations with the Greeks he was taken into the service of Eugenius IV and thus established himself. A little man, thin and ugly, intelligent and good-natured, he found himself in a position to realize the dream of his youth—to devote riches and power to books and monuments.

On the pontifical throne this profoundly pious priest, passionately devoted to St. Augustine, yet just as enthralled by the literature of antiquity, was now to demonstrate an unheard-of liberality in all those spheres where the Renaissance was at that moment flourishing. He decided to make Rome a permanent seat of Italian humanism, hitherto located principally in Florence. For this purpose he did not hesitate to change the entire character of the papal curia. From being monastic, he made it a centre of humanism.

In 1451 he brought in as his apostolic secretary Gianozzo Manetti, formerly the intimate of Eugene IV, who became the closest friend of the new pontiff. Manetti (d.1459) who had originally been employed in the service of Florence, was along with Ambrogio Traversari, the general of the Camaldolese, one of the finest types of Christian humanists in the first generation of the Renaissance.[7] He remained a layman, but was an excellent lay theologian (the first modern, no doubt, to have learnt Hebrew as an aid in his theological studies). His

7) cf. J. Burckhardt, *Civilization of the Renaissance in Italy* (New York : 1956), vol. I.

favourite books besides the Epistles of St. Paul, were the *City of God* and the *Nicomachean Ethics*. Nicholas V commissioned him to make a translation of the Bible from the Hebrew and Greek, and to prepare an apologetic dissertation against the Jews and pagans. But Manetti died too early to bring this immense work to completion. [8]

In retrospect, what is really extraordinary is the fact that Nicholas V had, along with Manetti, offered richly endowed situations in the curia to frankly pagan-minded humanists : to Poggio Bracciolini, author of the obscene *Facezie*, and to Filelfo, despite his invectives against monks. What seems even less believable is his employing Laurenzo Valla whom Eugenius IV had steadfastly refused to patronize. Valla, an excellent critic, had written a declamation *De Falsa Credita et Ementita Constantini Donatione* (*On the Falsely Believed and Lying Donation of Constantine*) the title of which sufficiently reveals its contents. How is this incredible tolerance to be explained ? It certainly cannot be laid to an error in the Pope's information, for the vices and opinions of these men were common knowledge. It can only be ascribed to a systematically liberal policy determined at all costs to take over the leadership of the humanist movement, and to disarm its more menacing tendencies by confidence and generosity.

From the beginning of the hellenistic phase of the Renaissance, the great concern of Nicholas V on the literary plane seems to have been to give the West easy access to both profane and patristic Greek literature. With that breadth of view characteristic

8) cf. the *Life* by Naldius Naldi in Muratori, *Scriptores Rerum italicarum*, XX, col. 532 ff. See also Vespasiano Bisticci, *Commentario della vita di Messer Gianozzo Manetti* publ. by Fanfani in his *Collegione di opere inedite o rare*, II (Turin : 1862).

of all his projects, the Pope organised a great work-shop for translations from Greek and Latin. On the one hand were to be found Homer, Herodotus, Thucydides, Xenophon, Polybius, Diodorus Siculus, Appian, Philo, Theophrastus, Ptolemy, and on the other, the *Praeparatio evangelica* of Eusebius, the Cappadocians, St. Cyril of Alexandria, these latter being entrusted to his intimate, Manetti. George of Trebizond was specially charged with the eighty homilies of St. John Chrysostom on St. Matthew. These vast enterprises were supported by the est-ablishment of the Vatican library, another creation of Nicholas V, for which he flooded the whole known world with his envoys and his gold.

But although this epoch exalted the humanists, and still considered the artists as little more than artisans,[9] the Pope's artistic projects were yet on a vast scale. Like all who achieve great things, he was most attracted to architecture, and looked upon the other arts, particularly painting, as useful in its service.[10] He decided to rebuild the Vatican palace. Following the counsel of Leone Battista, he was the first Pope who was not afraid to decide against the further repair of the Constantinian basilica of St. Peter, and to favour its complete replacement with a wholly new and grandiose church.[11]

After such a pontificate, it would seem impossible for the Renaissance to meet with a warmer acceptance on the part of any pope. And yet, after the short pontificate of Callixtus III (1455-1458), which was almost completely overshadowed by the renewed menace of the Turkish advance, that of Pius II

9) For the different treatment accorded the artist and the humanist, see Pastor, vol. I.

10) He brought Fra Angelico to Rome to have the walls of his office covered with frescoes.

11) Pastor, vol. I, pp. 1-258.

(1458-1464) offers an even more singular spectacle.

On the throne of St. Peter, Nicholas V had shown himself an amateur enthusiast of humanism. With Aeneas Sylvius Piccolomini it is a professional humanist who is seated there. Humanism has now become a genuine profession. It provides secretaries for the princes and gives positions to literary counsellors whose services can no longer be dispensed with.

Particularly as historiographers and as orators, the humanists now occupy an increasingly important position in all the institutions of the day.[12] It is to his exquisite command of Latin that Aeneas Sylvius owed his first position as secretary to the antipope Felix V, then his employment by the emperor Frederick III. Quite apart from his adhesion to the schism of Basel, he had not been in his youth what one would call an edifying author. But having undergone a true conversion, he had come to manifest in turn a horror for the pagan Renaissance. Yet in the end this did not prevent his adherence to humanism from being of a warmth and intimacy rare even among the specialists in the field. In order to form a proper idea of this it is necessary to read the letter he wrote Mohammed II at the time of the fall of Constantinople. As a prolongation of Greek antiquity which had been immobilized in its decline, Byzantium remained for him and his contemporaries a dream land. Thus is explained the sorrow he experienced in the face of this irremediable catastrophe. " Praecisus est fluvius omnium doctrinarum ; Musarum dessicatus est fons. Nunc Poesis, nunc Philosophia sepulta videtur," he had written to Nicholas of Cusa on the

12)   cf. the facts as reported by Burckhardt, *op.cit.*

21st of July 1453.[13]   At practically the same time
he wrote in a well-known letter to Pope Nicholas V :
" Secunda mors ista Homero est ;   secundus Platonis obitus."[14]

This destruction of the Byzantine civilization to
which he had been so attached was to prove an
omen which weighed heavily on the whole of his
reign. With a perception shared by too few of the
Christian princes, he had calculated the danger that
threatened a divided Christendom, as the Turks
made their way along the shores of the Mediterranean.
But in vain did he marshal his powers to inspire
a crusade that proved impossible. This effort of
his combined with his open hostility to neo-paganism
to disappoint somewhat the humanists who had
expected so much from his elevation. The chief
motive, however, behind a certain economy of
expenditure, was the very purity of his literary
and artistic taste. Certainly more critical and refined
than that of Nicholas V, this taste caused him to
say that " the post and the orator should be first-
rate, otherwise they are worthless."[15] Fond as he
was of manuscripts, he admitted but a limited number
of profane authors into his library. He was the first
to correct the style in the Latin letters of the curia
and to give them the Ciceronian turn which the
secretariat of briefs has kept ever since. He refrained,
however, from introducing too many innovations,
through fear of the doubts that might arise as to
the authenticity of the Bulls.

A patron of historians, among whom were Flavio

13)   " The flood of all wisdom has been stemmed. The fount of the Muse.
has run dry. First poetry, then philosophy has been buried " in his *Epistulae*
(ed. Nuremberg 1517, no. 155).

14)   " It is as if Homer had died a second death, it is as if Plato had died
again," Ibid, no. 162.

15)   cf. Pastor, vol .III.

Biondo (author of *Roma Triumphans*) and Ammanati (who wrote a history of the popes), and of the neo-Latin poets such as Giantonio Campano, the new Pope was himself engaged upon two immense works at the time of his election.[16]   One was an historical and geographical description of the then known world, of which he had only completed the first part, devoted to Asia. The other, under the title *Commentaria*, started as an autobiography, and contains extremely personal notes on great contemporary events and on his own deeds. It is here that he reveals the delicacy and originality of a profoundly religious man who was at the same time an artist and a poet. A careful and discerning love of beautiful scenery blends with sentiments roused by the Roman ruins which found lasting expression in a famous epigram of his, a foretaste, indeed, of du Bellay himself :

The sight of thy ruins, O Rome, is for
me a noble pleasure,
No delight can equal what your fallen
splendor gives.
But the glorious stones which they take
from your walls
Your people reduce to lime for miserable
gain.
Impious brood, if you persist, in three
hundred years
Not a trace of this ancient splendour
will be seen.[17]

His love for these ruins made of Pius II not only the protector of the monuments of ancient Rome but also the restorer of those of Christian Rome. His judgement in æsthetic matters was shown by

16) See Burckhardt, *op. cit.* vol. II.
17) The text is in Mabillon, *Museum ital.* vol. I, p. 97.

C

all the humanists in the Curia. His " victims "
did not suffer such a blow without unloosing against
the sovereign pontiff a flood of invective in keeping
with their usual style of polemic. But this time one
of the most celebrated among them, the neo-Latin
prose stylist Platina, paid with torture and a prolonged
imprisonment for a particularly violent letter which
he was bold enough to address to the Pope.

A second such incident occurred in 1468. It had
to do with the process brought against the members
of the famous Roman Academy. Was there a real
conspiracy, or did Paul II mistakenly exaggerate
the importance of these dreamers ? The matter
has never been cleared up. Be that as it may, a
group had been formed round Pomponius Laetus,
student and then successor to Valla at the University of
Rome, who attempted to resurrect Roman life as
it had been lived at the time of the republic. It seems
that this was no more than a literary pose, like the
mythology invading even that literature most Christian in inspiration. The academicians, however,
took their game so seriously as to consider themselves almost a pagan sacerdotal college. They
even began to indulge in customs worthy of the
ancients. Pomponius Laetus, shod in sandals and
dressed in Roman garments, used to gather his
friends for a philosophical banquet in his villa on
the Quirinal, or to cultivate his vineyard on the
Palatine, except when he was indulging in romantic
reveries among the ruins of the Forum. This is
but another example, following Gemistius Plethon,
of unconscious caricature, by way of imitation, of
the ancients. They demonstrate how far enthusiasm
for rediscoveries could go in its naivete.

But to come back to Paul II, in spite of his in-
terventions, he certainly was not the enemy of the

Renaissance as Platina was later to depict him. During his rule, the printing press, which was to enjoy such a rôle in the diffusion of humanism, was introduced into Italy. Conrad Schweinheim, of Schwanheim, and Arnold Pannartz of Prague, installed themselves first at Subiaco in 1465. From their presses came forth the *Grammar* of Donatus, the *De Oratore* of Cicero and the *Institutes* of Lactantius. When they came to Rome two years later, where their proof-reader was the humanist Bussi,[20] the Pope put the manuscripts of the Vatican at their disposal. Likewise in the domains of archaeology and of art, not only did Paul II actively pursue the restoration of the ancient monuments, but reconstructed the palace of Saint Mark. And it was he who laid the foundations for the present Vatican Museum which began with his incomparable collection of antiques.

20)   The bishop, and a friend of Nicholas of Cusa.

interested in the intellectual aspects of the movement, though he placed the decoration of the Belvedere in the hands of Pinturricchio and Mantegna, and asked Angelo Poliziano to translate into Latin the Greek historians of Ancient Rome.

But in the spring of 1485 a minor event took place which may be thought symbolic. It reveals very well the admiration the people of Rome had for the ancient world in these years. (The people of the times, it might be added, were not above embellishing the tale). Some masons had discovered the coffin of a young girl near the Appian Way. The inscription on the marble sarcophagus said simply : *Julia Claudii filia*—Julia, the daughter of Claudius. When opened, it was found to contain the body of a young girl of amazing beauty, wonderfully preserved. Brought into the capitol, it had such a bewitching effect on the whole town that Innocent VIII, in dismay, had it taken away at night and secretly buried beyond the Pincio.[5]

With the coming of Alexander VI, however, there is no need to say to what extent the fears silently expressed by Paul II were to show themselves justified. This time it was neither a Maecenas nor a humanist, but one of the most formidable adventurers of the Italian Renaissance, and a cosmopolitan, who ascended the pontifical throne, in the person of the Spaniard Rodrigo Borgia (1492-1503). Grandiose like his predecessors, and even devout, he covered the ceiling of St. Mary Major with the first gold brought back by Columbus, changed the Mausoleum of Hadrian into the Castel Sant' Angelo, founded the leonine city planned by Nicholas V, and commissioned Pinturricchio to decorate the appartments which bear his name.

5) cf. Burckhardt, *Civilization of the Renaissance in Italy*, vol. I.

Meanwhile, he re-organized the university of Rome and, himself a jurist, gathered about him men of learning and letters.

Paradoxical as it may seem, it is during his reign that the first decree censoring books dangerous to faith and morals was issued. But it must be admitted that never had Christian civilization appeared to be so close to being annihilated at its very source, by a revivified paganism. There were times when, with the knowledge of the Pope, his son, Caesar Borgia, the model for Machiavelli's prince, acted as if he considered the sovereign pontificate a hereditary acquistion, and when the Vicar of Christ was out of Rome for a few days, instructed the secretaries to take orders for rescripts not from the cardinals, but from " Madonna Lucrezia," the Pope's daughter.

This epoch seemed bent upon proving in advance Macaulay's remark that the Catholic Church had come out of so many mortal crises alive that there was simply no telling what could kill her. [6]

In this third phase of the papacy's relations with the Renaissance, Alexander VI by the excess of his nepotism was to cause a new reaction. Yet the renewal of confidence due to Sixtus IV was not by any means belied. Pope Julius II (1503-1513)— after the brief interval of Pius III who only reigned for a single month of agony—liberated the papacy for a time from the yoke of nepotism. He restored the temporal dignity of the sovereign pontificate, which under the Borgias had degenerated to an almost complete identification with the other Italian principalities. Nevertheless he is the first pope of the Renaissance forced to face, in the Italian wars, not indeed an enemy from without, such as the

6)   cf. Pastor, vol. V & VI.

unique care was to please and to be himself pleased, was never conscious of the gravity of his position, nor of the rôle in which he had to acquit himself.

The years of his reign saw Italian art continue to flourish as it had under Julius II. They witnessed too, the sudden maturation of the strictly intellectual side of the Renaissance. The time of rapture over the first discoveries had passed, and imitation of the literature of antiquity became less intelligent and more formalized. By then there was a considerable number of men who had read, assimilated, and criticized the enormous deposit of pre-mediaeval thought, whose original content the preceding generations had assiduously labored to restore. The moment had come to integrate this deposit with the traditional treasure of Catholicism, and at the same time to give the faith a new expression, to adjust Catholic life to a wholly different setting. Here could have been secured that great enrichment of Christian civilization that Erasmus, Thomas More, Sadoleto, and the better minds of the age, looked for and desired.

But it is likewise here that Christian civilization was running the most grave risks. For its very spirit was jeopardized by the attempt to refashion its whole tradition and ways of thinking and living. The development of humanism—in France with Lefèvre d'Étaples and in Germany especially with Reuchlin, the reviver of Hebrew studies—and then with Erasmus—quickly oriented itself in the direction of the sacred sciences. In this way it brought on a crisis that gave it a new and primarily theological colouring.

To dominate this situation and to move it in a salutary direction, something more than the universal good will and superficial eclecticism of a

Leo X was called for. In one period of barely two years this pontiff accepted the dedication of an edition of the Cabala by Reuchlin, and also that of a book which Hochstraten wrote against it.[8] And this example is typical. Leo X turned a kindly face to all the world, and his court brought together the greatest names of Italy : in the arts there were Raphael, Bramante, Michelangelo, Peruzzi, the two Sansovinos, Julian and Anthony de Sangalla, Sodoma, Sebastiano del Piombo, Fra Giocondo ; in letters, Bibbiena, Bembo, Sadoleto, Castiglione, Carpi, Giovio, Lascaris. His circle of protégés was even more extensive. But just as an Ariosto was lost in the crowd of mediocre poets, all rewarded with the indiscriminate bounty of the Pope, so not even the profoundly Christian humanism of a Sadoleto was distinguished from the elegance, frivolous even at this date, of a Bembo. The intimate friend and confidant of the Pope was the scandalous Cardinal Bibbiena, who is famous for two things— the sumptuously sensuous paintings in his baths ornamented with the drawings of Raphael, and the obscenity of *La Calandra*, a comedy he wrote and which the Pope did not hesitate to have performed in his presence.

All this indicates lack of firm judgement, proceeding from a want of firmness of character. Life for this Medici was nothing but a continual worldly festival of which he was the hero. It was to perpetuate this atmosphere around him, rather than as a truly enlightened patron of art that the pope laid a heavy hand on the Church's treasury. At the same time, he caused increasing disquiet by surrounding the throne of St. Peter with an aristocracy of money—especially the Chigi and the Strozzi, upon

8) Pastor, vol. VIII.

phase, the first real reaction, is at hand.[11]

If what happened under Paul II hardly deserved
to be called a reaction, what began in January, 1522
with Adrian IV (1522-1523) was quite different.
Adrian Florensz, born at Utrecht, educated like
Erasmus by the Brothers of the Common Life, and
teacher at the university of Louvain, had been the
tutor of Charles V. Elevated by the Emperor to
the cardinalate and to the vice-royalty of Spain,
he found himself suddenly elected, as in desperation,
to bring to a close the interminable conclave that
he had not even taken the trouble to attend. No
sooner was he elected than the Italian cardinals
quickly repented they had even thought of the studious Dutchman. But it was too late. Hardly had he
arrived in Rome, than he commenced by refusing
to grant any preferment, banished all prostitutes
from the city, and ordered the priests to shave off
their beards. Coming into the Sistine Chapel, he
gave one look at the ceiling painted by Michelangelo
and asked simply if it was the bathroom. Leo's
vast domestic staff was dismissed, and replaced
by an old Dutch housekeeper to do his mending.
All this upset the Romans considerably.

Though he showed not the slightest interest in
Italian art, Adrian IV was not the barbarian that
he was once alleged to be. He thought little of
the poets and the bands of humanists, but showed
judgement in his regard for Erasmus, and Sadoleto
too. But he had the Belvedere walled up, keeping
the keys in his own pocket. And turning his back
on all that had enchanted Leo X, he attempted to
tackle in a serious manner the most urgent task
—to stop the Protestant Revolt, and to that end
bring about at last a real reform of the Curia

11) See Pastor, vol. VIII.

itself.   Less than two years after his election, he died with his task hardly started[12].

12)   Pastor, vol. IX.

CHAPTER IV

INDIAN SUMMER

AFTER ADRIAN IV began a fifth and last phase, as it were the autumn of the Renaissance. Under Clement VII (1523-1534)—Giulio de Medici, nephew of Leo X,—it started with a simple repetition on a smaller scale of the latter's policy. But Clement did not possess the artistic qualities of his uncle. Nor, on the other hand, had he inherited Leo's incessant need of pleasure. He gathered round him once again the same artists and men of letters, but seemed to manifest more discernment of real merit by allotting to such men as Giberti and Sadoleto important posts in the government of the Church, as well as by the intelligent protection he extended to Erasmus (through papal letters in 1524 and 1537). He was equally favourable to Copernicus, whose system had begun to revolutionize men's minds. Yet despite all this he pursued the same liberal policy towards those humanist writers whose intentions were irreconcilable with the Church, Guicciardini, Machiavelli, Giovio, and even such frivolous poets as Firenzuola and Berni. Even the base Aretino was in favour with him for a time.

Yet all this was but the last flaring up of a bonfire on the point of extinction. In 1527 as a result of Clement's continual scheming among the different powers, there came a sudden catastrophe which, like a flash of lighting, ended the Italian Renaissance on the instant—this was the sack of Rome by the Imperial troops. While the Pope, who escaped by a miracle, was being besieged in the Castel Sant'

Angelo, the international soldiery gave itself over not merely to a disgraceful pillage of the city, but to a series of crimes of monstrous savagery. These horrible incidents throw a revealing light on the paganization of the masses of the people, which was the sad concomitant of the new culture and of the resulting religious confusion.

After this nightmare, the survivors of the Roman Renaissance were never themselves again. In the correspondence of Michelangelo with the poetess, Vittoria Colonna, there is a certain, sad sense of an irremediable loss—the great Christian hope entered upon in the springtime of the Renaissance had passed the time of its flowering, and brought forth now nothing but bitter fruits.[1] The fine, so human dream of the first years in Florence is no more. The last survivor of a dying generation, the Michelangelo of the final years was to replace this dream with the terrifying apocalypse of his " Last Judgement." The last days of this irresolute and now lethargic pontificate saw the English schism complete the disaster of the Reformation, which the other Medicis had not known how to forestall or avert.[2]

In 1534, after another interminable conclave, began the pontificate of Paul III (1534-1549), which was to be, in many ways, so startling. Alexander Farnese had been elected when at the point of death, in order that time might be gained for agreement on a more stable successor. But instead of dying after a few weeks, as had been expected, he lived another fifteen years—the longest pontificate of the century. A talented politician, conscious of the risks he ran with his irascible temper, he had till then always managed to speak with a low tone of

1) cf. H. Grimm, *Michel-Ange et son temps* (Paris, 1934), pp. 430 ff.
2) Pastor, vol. IX.

voice. But once in power, he exhibited inflexible authority. This persistent sensualist, who, made a cardinal under the Borgias, had kept his mistress in his palace until 1513, once seated upon the papal throne, not only continued his recent habits of piety and austerity, but was the first pope seriously intent on reform. In 1540, he approved the foundation of the Jesuits and in 1545 he at last convoked the Council of Trent.

The great historical interest of this pontificate for us, however, is that Paul III, in setting about his reform, far from breaking with the Renaissance, made a final attempt to enlist its support. What he did, in fact, was to entrust the work to the best among the Christian humanists, those in other words who had separated out all the postive gains of this troubled epoch,—to Sadoleto whom he rescues from exile in the far-away bishopric of Carpentra, Contarini, and Pole.

Elevated to the cardinalate along with Caraffa, these men were to draw up a draft of the *Concilium de emendanda Ecclesia*—Council for Reforming the Church—under the presidency of Contarini in 1536. It is impossible to re-read this plan for reform without regretting the fact that the circumstances of the time did not allow a number of these projects to get further than paper. For a last time, at the end of an epoch so fertile in disillusions and catastrophes, there appears the same largeness of view, the same eirenic approach as had animated Eugene IV and Pius II. Contarini's embassy to the Ratisbon Conversations is most significant in this respect. The hope of restoring the unity of Christendom, of putting a reform into effect not indeed against the Protestants but along with them persisted, though even then it appeared overbold. There was too, a continual and tenacious attempt to regain leadership in the development men's minds were undergoing, instead of setting dead against it. The prospect arose of a Christian civilization emerging from this immense crisis not only intact but matured and re-animated in its recovered unity.[3]

It turned out to be nothing but a beautiful dream. Nevertheless, it seemed on the verge of realization when the papal throne was offered to Cardinal Pole in 1550. Had it not been for a conscientious scruple which caused him to refuse the election made by a simple acclamation, we should have had the extraordinary spectacle of a pope who was a great English noble and cousin to Henry VIII. What is more, one of the most perfect examples of a man formed by humanism, who was at the same time an irreproachable Christian, and whose mother had been martyred, would have had the direction of the Church precisely when it had the most crucial decisions to make.

All the same, it is when we come upon opportunities of this sort, lost apparently by chance, that a law of history established by Carnot comes to mind[4] : exceptional individuals do indeed occasion considerable stir on the surface of history ; but they cannot prevail for long against the general tendencies of the masses if these latter will not go along with them. The protestant Reformation was by then not only too far advanced but too thoroughly at enmity with the Church, without being as yet disappointed in its own aspirations, to have put much stock in reconciliation. Furthermore, Catholicism itself was no longer possessed

3) Pastor. vol XI and XII.

4) *Considérations sur la marche des idées et des événements*, (Paris : new ed., 1934) vol. I, pp. 10 ff.

of, nor had it regained, sufficient vitality to take on
the risk of so generous a policy. Whatever the
result, it was obliged to be firm in order not to yield.
A liberal policy followed for so long without any
counter-balance had by now allowed the gangrene
of a renascent paganism to corrupt the body. There
could be no doubt, particularly after the sack of
Rome, and in the bewildering atmosphere revealed
in the autobiography of Benvenuto Cellini, that
the Christian Renaissance had on the whole failed
disastrously, despite the brilliant exceptions of men
like Sadoleto, Contarini, and Pole. Besides, even
these men, however well-intentioned their efforts,
suffered from the lack of a strict theology, or simply
of a firm religious philosophy. It was a lack congenital to the Renaissance, as we have suggested.

This can be seen in their unfortunate theory of a
two-fold justification, engineered to regain the
Protestants, but at the price of unconscious equi-
vocations. Now it was at this very moment that
the reformed neo-Christianity came on the scene.
In Italy, the most edifying among the popular
preachers of Catholic reform had one after the other
passed over to the enemy with a disturbing facility. [5]
And it was then too that the great intellectual
prelates made their attempt to disarm the enemy
by an eirenic approach that was not sufficiently
on its guard. The fears provoked by the paradoxical danger seem to have precipitated an inevitable reaction. This time, the movement of recoil
was so impetuous that not only did this century-old
ecclesiastical liberalism disappear for good, but
the Church was to retain in its regard so severe
and readily suspicious an attitude as had never
been since the beginning of the age of Constantine.

5)   Pastor, vol XII, pp. 303 ff.

All the same the pontificate of Julius III (1550-1555) attempted one last artificial strategem characteristic of the Renaissance. It happened that, after a series of normal delays, Pole was summoned from his retreat at Viterbo—that supreme centre whence Christian humanism shed its last and purest rays—and was hustled off on that intriguing and useless adventure of the English legation. It had met with an astonishing success in the beginning, for in 1557, he absolved from schism and heresy both the Queen and the two houses of parliament kneeling at his feet in Westminster. Perhaps he might have been able to heal a whole section of the great schism of the century. But death was to interrupt the work which had begun so auspiciously.

Yet it is possible that this premature death prevented an even more dramatic catastrophe. In 1555, Julius III himself died. After the three months of the pontificate of Marcellus II, Cardinal Caraffa, as Paul IV (1555-1559), who become more and more hardened in his reactionary tendencies, succeeded to the pontifical throne. The inner reform of the Church, until then pursued with a tolerance bordering on indolence, was attacked with new energy. But at the same time, the uncompromising rigidity of his manner was sudden and harsh in its effects. The temporal policy of the new pope unhappily intensified the effect of his rigorousness and, it must be admitted, of a certain inhumanity in his actions and proceedings that was, as it were, the nemesis of the too human humanism of Leo X and so many others. For the new pope grew suspicious of all the saints of the counter-reform, one after the other—of St. Ignatius as well as of St. Philip Neri. Paul IV went so far as to include in the first catalogue of the Index a work of Cardinal Caraffa

himself. It was the report of the famous commission
de emendanda Ecclesia. It is not surprising, then, that
Pole, on the point of leaving both his life and his
work in England so well begun had the painful
sense that he had forfeited, though undeservedly,
the Pope's trust. [6]

This tragic misunderstanding is symbolic. The
Renaissance, purged and baptised, dies from the
excesses of the pagan renaissance. The papacy
which did not withdraw the confidence it had placed
in it even in the hours of its aberrations, had to
leave it in turn. We might be tempted to think
that it finally abandoned the Renaissance at the very
moment when the latter was making ready to return
and to make resitution for the losses it had caused.
But here once more it is necessary to recall the
remarks of Cournot. The Christian urbanity of a
Pole could not mend the seamless cloak, nor did
the narrowness, or what one might call the fanaticism,
of Caraffa really help on the inevitable revolution.
Promising as had been the work of Pole, the times
were not suited for it. Favourable occasions, when
great numbers of the people might have followed,
had long since been lost, when there appeared this
handful of men—Sadoleto, Contarini, Pole—who,
had they arrived earlier, would have been able to
attract others. What this means is simply that the
carelessness, the levity, the lack of vision, and particularly the disagreement of minds had let the
moment escape in which the Christian civilization
of the Middle Ages might have reasserted itself
after a crisis in its growth and been splendidly
renewed. In any case, the amiable, too amiable
indeed, countenance of Christianity under Sixtus

6) On Pole's legation, see Pastor, vol. XIII and XIV. For Pope Paul IV,
see vol. XIV.

IV was to find itself replaced by the sternness of post-tridentine Christianity. It was hard for many to resign themselves to it, but there was no other alternative but death.

BOOK II

HUMANIST THEOLOGY—

FROM NICHOLAS OF CUSA TO
THE PRAISE OF FOLLY

WE HAVE OBSERVED the manner in which the traditional institution for the harmony and preservation of Christian civilization behaved in face of the disturbing influences so quickly penetrating medieval society in the fifteenth century. The development of the papal attitude toward the Renaissance has shown us what may be termed the social reaction of Christianity in respect to humanism. Now we are to approach the same matter from the opposite direction. We no longer consider how the Church's authorities, looking at it from outside and above, acted towards an autonomous movement, but rather how, immersed in the movement from within and carried along in its course, certain outstanding personalities attempted to live in the humanist experiment as real Christians, and at the same time, to accord their Christian experience with humanism,

Our new subject for study can be called the theology of the humanists. We have no intention here of speaking of a formal dogmatic theology, with which the humanists were certainly not greatly concerned. We have the rather more modest one of considering how these Christians attempted to rethink their faith and their lives with the aid of new materials provided for them by the ideas and achievements of their age. There is no question here of attempting to furnish a complete study. We must content ourselves with singling out in the course of the development of the Renaissance certain representative personalities in each phase who will serve our purpose.

We pause first at the end of the Middle Ages to consider one of the men who certainly was in advance of his own times. Cardinal Nicholas of Cusa shows the nature of the first encounter of the spirit of

mediaeval civilization with the new spirit that was
to result in the Renaissance. Then we hope to spend
a little time discussing the serene and fine personality
of Vittorino da Feltre, one of the great pedagogues
who are to be met with at the origin of humanism,
not only in so far as it was a movement of learned
men, but as a human ideal. We will see in him how,
from the beginning of the Renaissance, the great
work of supernatural education which the medieval
civilization had proposed as its objective tried to
recast itself in view of the new disciplines of learning
and of the new spirit.

In the engaging figure of Pico della Mirandola
we will be able to examine one of the first typical
examples of this education which was at once traditional and renewed. Thereby we discover the youth,
as it were, of that new man, the Christian humanist.
In Pico we can admire the fascinating exuberance
and the ephemeral brilliance of this youth ; but we
perceive, too, its lack of balance and internal dis-
sension. With Erasmus we come to the maturity
of the same type of Christian humanist. We admire
in him the harmonious combination of many diverse
elements ; but attacks of discouragement, lack of
persistence, withdrawal into self, which are so
liable to occur in a maturity following a most
promising adolescence, are none the less apparent.

Behind the figure of Erasmus, we see emerging
the pure, truly great figure of a man who at least
knew how to realise and surpass in his maturity
the apparently wild dreams of his youth. It is that
of a saint—the saint of humanism—the most intimate, perhaps the only true friend of Erasmus :
Sir Thomas More.

After that we will come to the old age of this
ideal of Christian humanism which we have seen

born and growing in the course of the fifteenth and
sixteenth centuries. This luminous old age, wherein
are gathered the treasures of the early days, tried
and found true amid the vicissitudes of daily life,
is depicted in the group of theologians to whom
Pope Paul III entrusted the elaboration of the
Consilium de emendanda Ecclesia—we single out
from them the three cardinals : Pole, Contarini, and
Sadoleto. But here it is obvious that the sources
are drying up, and that the time of renewal has passed,
that even the mental vigour, still present, begins
to feel itself precarious. The type is on the verge
of disappearing, not through destruction, but through
alteration. The humanist Christian, in whom
medieval civilization had attempted in the course
of the Renaissance to renew and prolong its own
existence, in reality outlived it. Another, a different
type, comes to replace him, which by way of contrast we can designate the Christian humanist.

We can see him coming to the fore in the immediate entourage of Paul III's cardinals, in the
personality of Balthasar Castiglione. It is in him, in
his famous book called *The Courtier*, that we discover a principal source of the immense influence
brought to bear on the French Renaissance. Here
is where we discern the first traits of the baroque
civilization which lies at the basis of our classical
culture. How does it come about that this other
new man, who is a completely different synthesis
of the same materials, so quickly displaces the new
man of the Renaissance which thought itself
Christian? In attempting to find an answer to this
final question, we may be able to explain how the
theology in which the Renaissance had expressed
its humanist Christianity was merely a momentary
flame, to die almost as soon as it was kindled.

In such a study Erasmus will take the lion's share. He stands at the centre of the whole field of vision, and at the summit of its development. On the interpretation given to his theological essay depends in large measure our understanding of the Christian Renaissance.

CHAPTER V

NICHOLAS OF CUSA

Born at Kues (Cusa), between Trier and Coblenz, in 1401, the son of a boatman on the Moselle, Nicholas Krebs[1] retained so close an attachment to his native land that his memory is still cherished there. He had founded and organized a hospice there which is only comparable to the celebrated hostels in Beaune. Following rules which he himself had minutely laid down, life went on there right up to the eve of World War II in the very buildings he had erected, where the books, the astronomical instruments, and the personal effects of the learned cardinal are devotedly preserved in the state in which he had left them. [2]

This fact is all the more touching because Nicholas of Cusa, more by the breadth of his interests and of his contacts than by his journeys, was to be one of the first exemplars of the cosmopolitanism of the Renaissance.

Like Erasmus a little later, he seems to have been a student of the Brothers of the Common Life at

1) On Nicholas of Cusa there are two voluminous studies, both recent and of similar scientific quality. The first is that of Edmond Vansteenberghe, *Le Cardinal Nicholas de Cuse* (1401-1464), (Paris, 1920) primarily a biography. But it includes a resumé of his extraordinary original system, which in itself gives evidence of an almost impenetrable obscurity. The same author has another essay on the subject : *Autour de la docte ignorance, une controverse sur la théologie mystique au XVe siècle* (Munster-in-Westphalia, 1914), a monograph that reveals the heart of the system of Nicholas of Cusa.
cf. M. Maurice Patronnier de Gandillac, *La philosophie de Nicolas de Cuse* (in Lavelle et Le Senne, *Philosophie de l'esprit* [Paris : 1941]).

2) cf. de Gandillac, *op. cit.*, p. 35.

Deventer where his patron, the Count of Manderscheid, had him enrolled.   In the spring of 1416, he
went to the university of Heidelberg.

This was the moment in which the Great Schism
broke out in full fury.   In 1415 the decrees of the
Council of Constance had been passed, affirming
the superiority of a general council over the pope.
In 1417 (the year in which the election of Pope
Martin V put an end to the schism if not to the
controversies) Nicholas of Cusa went to Padua to
study law.   The university there was distinguished
by the teaching of the jurist Cesarini, whose pupil
Nicholas became in 1421.   But he did not confine
himself to such studies.   It was in these years that
his universal curiosity was revealed and gratified.
He was initiated into mathematics and astronomy
under Prosdoscimo de' Beldomandi, and had for
a fellow student the man who was to be the most
learned of the century, Paolo del Pozzo Toscanelli.

In 1423, Nicholas received his doctorate in canon
law.   He was still studying in 1425, but this time
theology at Cologne.   He had, moreover, won some
distinction among the humanists.   In 1426 as secretary to the papal legate Orsini, he took advantage
of his journeys to do research work in the various
monastic libraries.   His first reward was the discovery of one of the most complete manuscripts
of Plautus.   Meanwhile he had become a priest,
canon of Saint Simeon's cathedral in Trier, and
then dean of St. Florent of Coblenz.

The first decisive step in his future career, however,
as well as in the unfolding of his " system " was
taken in 1431, in the course of a commission entrusted to him by his patron Ulric of Manderscheid.
At the Council of Basel he was charged with presenting the claims of Ulric to the archepiscopal see of

Trier. This was done against the interests of a candidate named by the Holy See. Having arrived at the council, towards the end of 1432, Nicholas of Cusa entered enthusiastically into the movement of ideas, controversies, and research brought about by this gathering of the most prominent humanists and theologians of the day. He quickly distinguished himself, passing to the first ranks among the gathering. A partisan of the council at first, he lost his case, but his experience of conciliar anarchy quickly brought about a change in his loyalties. Consequently he joined the minority, at the head of whom he found his old master, Cesarini.

In 1433, the very personal theology of his *De concordantia catholica* revealed his adhesion to the papal party. But it showed too the kind of peacemaking effort on which he would thereafter spend all his time and thought. For him, adherence to the principle of the pope's superiority over a council did not require a pure and simple rejection of the concept of the Church held by the conciliar advocates. Rather he attempted to collect all the positive elements in each system and to bring them together in a superior synthesis. Whatever one may think of this theology, so personal, as was indeed the whole of his thought, one cannot help being impressed by the powerful ideas of the young theologian.

Nicholas of Cusa deals successively with the general constitution of the Church, with what he called its soul, that is the priesthood, and its body, the Holy Roman Empire. As the title he chose for the work indicates, the principle aim of the book is to determine under what conditions this soul and this body should be able to unite harmoniously, in order to assure at once the eternal and the temporal

welfare of the Christian people. [3] The most interesting
point in all this is the concept of the Church held
by Nicholas. He calls it a " brotherhood," and he
gives it this definition : " The union of souls with
Christ in sweet harmony." [4] But far from opposing
this notion to that of a hierarchial Church, he
shows how there is in the hierarchy a necessary
means for assuring what he terms " a connecting
order " between all the parts of the Church, an
orderly transmission of the " power " emanating
from Christ and passing through all Christians thus
joined together, like the attractive force of a magnet. [5]
He tries to demonstrate the same continuity in the
Church Militant, the Church Suffering, and the
Church Triumphant, all three tending together
toward a universal union with God. [6] As in heaven
there is the Trinity, the angels and the blessed,
so on earth there is the sacramental order in which
the priests help the faithful to participate. Actually,
he seeks to discover a connecting link between the
sacraments themselves which in his thought would
be comparable to that between the divine persons.
And in the priestly hierarchy, he seeks an analogy
of the heavenly hierarchy. [7] In each diocese, the
bishop is essentially an agent for unity, and represents
in himself the whole Church. It is the same with
regard to the pope's relation to the universal Church,
which is of such a nature that, he says, Catholics
must of necessity adhere to the papacy if they desire
to remain among the faithful. [8]

3)   Vansteenberghe, *Nicholas de Cuse*, p.35.
4)   Book I, chap. I and V.
5)   Ibid, chap. II.
6)   Ibid, chap. V.
7)   Ibid, chap. VI and VIII.
8)   Ibid, chap. XIV-XVII, cf. also Vansteenberghe, *op. cit.* p. 36. The influence of St. Ignatius of Antioch and of St. Irenaeus is noticeable in the foregoing formulas, but they are used in an original fashion. The basis of his
thought seems to be Dionysian.

That same year, Nicholas of Cusa became involved in negotiations with the Hussites. He found himself forced for the first time to put into practice the firmly unitary and yet largely conciliatory political action advocated in his theory. Pope Eugene IV was quick to distinguish and employ so remarkable a personality.

In 1437 took place the event which seems to have stirred him to the keenest enthusiasm and given him the strongest encouragement to realise the grand vision of Catholic unity which dominated him from then on. In the name of the minority of the Council of Basel and with the approbation of the pope, he made the journey to Constantinople, and brought back as far as Venice John Paleologus and the Greek patriarch for the council planned by Pope Eugene IV to heal the division of East and West.

The new council opened at Ferrara, on April 4, 1428. It was later transferred to Florence where, on July 5, 1439, in the Church of St. Mary of the Flowers, the union of the two Churches was proclaimed.

During these memorable days, the ideals and ideas that stimulated the mind of Nicholas of Cusa met and joined as a single force. The union of the Western Church, the reunion of the Greek and Latin Churches, the discovery among the Byzantines of a still-living hellenic antiquity, the prospect of an entire, unknown world and of a new unification of thought far wider and loftier than any of those attempted so far, all these things opened up before him at this moment. In the middle of the Adriatic, on the galley " Bucentaurus," in the brilliant decorations prepared by Venice for the Emperor and the Patriarch—Nicholas experienced something of an illumination. He saw in a flash the whole body of principles on which his later work would attempt to assemble and co-ordinate all these numerous data in a marvellous personal synthesis.

This " system " appeared in 1440 in an essay called " *De Docta Ignorantia.*" The numerous productions which followed were merely a ceaseless reworking of the same fundamental concept, giving it various applications and covering the entire field of philosophy and theology. Ten years later, in a dialogue called *The Idiot*, he once again expressed his original intuition in a familiar form, and with a precision that gives finality to his thought.

It is extremely difficult to give a brief idea of this philosophy without caricaturing it. We are dealing with a body of thought in which we detect numerous historical affiliations, and in particular the influences of Eckhart and of the neo-Platonists— although it is only in 1453 that Nicholas comes to know Proclus. Yet the whole gives the impression of being merely an alien element intruding in the history of Christian thought. Nicholas has been considered the father of that German idealism which runs from Leibniz to Schilling, but it is the "existentialist " philosophers of the last twenty years who are more closely related to his underlying intentions. According to de Gandillac, it would seem that the key to his system is furnished by the bizarre mathematical speculations which he so frequently indulged. Though these may be considered as preparing the way for modern mathematics, and particularly for all that concerns the differential and integral calculus, the principal interest of such studies, for us as well as for their author, remains chiefly philosophic. One problem especially never ceased to trouble him : that of the infinite and its relation to the finite. On this point, his thought seems to be a dialectic of immanence and transcendence. It proceeds wholly from an analysis of the intuitive faculty of the human spirit. It is evidently on this account that the title " father of idealism " which has been bestowed on him, seems to have some justification. Nevertheless there is nothing more paradoxical than the complexity of this philosophy which is so dedicated to unity, a " catholic " unity indeed, able to bind together all the strands of reality, without losing or impairing a single one.

What appeared to him as eminently characteristic of the finite spirit was the strange fact that in all its activities it demands the infinite. This was to be understood in two senses, each inseparable from the other.

In the first place, the notion that he formed of the spirit was wholly dynamic. Whenever we look deeply into any particular idea, according to him, we come upon a whole world of interconnected ideas, ultimately reaching the infinite. All is in all, and the individual cannot attain perfect knowledge of himself other than by attaining perfect knowledge of all that exists. It is this *coincidentia oppositorum* that is the most disturbing part of his system, but also that most dear to the author. We can see immediately how this becomes the epistemological principle of his universal eirenicism, both on the religious and the philosophic plane. We see too that it cannot in any way be understood in a static sense, and that it is absolutely unthinkable as an identification of logical contradictories. What it does contain is a dynamic sense of the reciprocal implications in what seems in reality to be most heterogeneous.

But this is only the first stage of the system. At this level, it appears that each element of the world,

in the very fact that it is itself and seems to offer
opposition to all else that is, is in reality ceaselessly
tending towards absorption in all the rest, continually in motion but never able to reach its end. It
is precisely here that we should observe that
Nicholas's metaphysical intuition led him to the
verge of those mathematical notions which Leibniz
was to introduce as the basis for his differential
calculus. On the other hand, the fact that he grew
in awareness of himself and his being as he grew in
awareness of all that was not himself and of his
necessary relation to this virtual infinity, is inseparable from this other consideration of his that the
finite spirit must recognize that in so far as it is
itself actual, it likewise postulates an actual infinity.

It is here that we pass to the second stage, which is
no longer that of the reciprocal implication of the
individual and of the world with their conjointly
unlimited becoming, but of what is implied in the
reality of becoming itself, and in the reality of God.
How is this higher mode of implication to be understood ? Precisely by what Nicholas of Cusa means
by " learned ignorance", that is to say by the intuitive discovery of the beyond, a thing more real
than everything else, stretching back behind the
limitless progress of what the mind is able to know,
and presupposed by this progress itself. Hence
the term "learned ignorance" ; for it is only by
escaping beyond the perpetually receding limits
of normal knowledge, that is by renouncing knowledge in the usual sense of the word, that the mind
comes to know God. Philosophy thus issues in
mysticism. [9]

The fact is that without being a mystic himself,
Nicholas looked to the mystics of the Rhineland

9)　For all this, see de Gandillac, *op.cit*. pp. 116 ff. and 182 ff.

for the spiritual foundation of his system. Besides, as Mgr. Vansteenberghe has well demonstrated in his study *Autour de la Docte Ignorance* the Cusan must have seized upon the first opportunity offered to verify his system in some way, by drawing from it a theory of mystical contemplation. The opportunity was given him by the controversy his diocesans the monks of the Tegernsee, Bernard of Wagnys and John of Weilheim, had with the Carthusian Vincent of Aggsbach.

At the very moment when Nicholas of Cusa was elaborating his speculation, his transcendent metaphysics joined in a curious partnership with a realistic politics to make him, first at the Diet of Mainz in 1441 and then in 1442 at Frankfurt, the active protagonist of the Pope against Cardinal John Aleman. It is extremely interesting and curious to see him apply the principles of his metaphysic in an attempt at the reconciliation of these irresolute partisans of Basel with the papacy. In his letter of May 20, 1442 to Sanchez d'Arevalo, orator of King Rodrigo of Castille, he sums up his thought on the pope and the Church, saying that the pope in his unity " implicates " the whole church, and that the Church, in which the multitude of believers " shares in otherness the unity of the same faith," is, as it were, an ' explanation,' in the etymological sense, or development, if the term be preferred, of Peter himself.[10]

The role played by Nicholas of Cusa in destroying the schism resulted in his elevation to the cardinalate in 1448, with the titular church of St. Peter in Chains, soon after the election of Pope Nicholas V. It was like an immediate reward for the agreement which he had negotiated between the papacy and the

10)   Edition of Basel, pp. 825-29.

Empire, the year before. The Emperor's representative in the discussion had been a friend of his, the hellenist Aeneas Sylvius. In a few years, by a strange reversal of rôles, Aeneas Sylvius as Pope Pius II was to make Nicholas vicar in matters temporal. Nicholas spent the whole of the year 1450-51 in an important mission which took him to all the countries of the Empire. He was able to bring about the pacification called for as a result of the Great Schism, and established throughout the foundations of what might have been a vigorous reform of the clergy. During Eastertide, 1452, he took possession of his bishopric at Brixen in the Tyrol. He tried to set a good example by staying in residence ; and, doubtless, he hoped to be able to pursue his favourite studies in the relative solitude of a provincial city. But the very instant that saw him at the summit of his career saw the splendid period of his life with all the wonderful possibilities in the intellectual sphere that seemed to open out before him begin to decline. His firm confidence in a total reconciliation between reality, enlarged by recent discovery, and the traditional faith, was to suffer its first and, perhaps, severest rebuff from that very reality.

He was pulled up sharp by the increasing emancipation of the temporal power from subjection to the medieval Church, at the very time when the Renaissance, intensifying this process, was turning it into revolt. A minor difference he had with the Abbess of Sonnenburg (he had demanded the reform of her monastery) was to serve as pretext for a conflict of a much greater consequence with Duke Sigismund of the Tyrol.

In the Duke's entourage, from 1458, there appeared a lawyer named Gregory Heimberg, a kind of German Machiavelli, whose anti-ecclesiastical and anti-Christian political theories formed an exact counterpart of Nicholas's eirenicism. But it was in 1437 that he underwent his worst experience. Barely escaping a sudden attack, Nicholas had to leave his episcopal see and take refuge in his chateau at Andraz. "It was a marvellous retreat for a romantic soul," writes Mgr. Vansteenberghe, "for in the rare atmosphere of these high altitudes there shoot up above a range of dazzling glaciers strange pyramids of red limestone gilded and reddened by the sun's rays."[11]

One can easily imagine the contrast between the meditations of the disillusioned Nicholas, pursued into this eagle's nest, and the philosophic ecstasy he had only recently enjoyed on the duke's galley in the calm of the Adriatic. After facing the peril with persistent courage, Nicholas, weary but unconquered, retired to Rome in 1459. At the end of a year, soon after the election of Pope Pius II, he tried once more to affirm with his episcopal authority the claim of the Church against the pretensions of a temporal power at once disrespectful and predatory. But his own diocesan chapter abandoned him, so he gave up. In 1461, Pius II excommunicated Gregory Heimberg. But both Nicholas and the Pope had in the end to consent to a political peace with Sigismund for fear of the menace of the Turks.

It is worth noting that only twenty years after the Hussite conflict Nicholas of Cusa was obliged first to attack the emancipating tendencies of the Renaissance, and then to abandon the struggle. In the previous struggle, on the other hand, it was to St. John Capistran's ecclesiastical authoritarianism that he had been opposed. Events had moved rapidly. Christian liberalism, though highly

11) Vansteenberghe, *op. cit.* p. 180.

flexible and open to new ideas, was forced to adopt
in its turn an attitude of intransigence. But the
pressure was already too strong for such barriers
to hold up.

It makes it still more touching to see
Nicholas, in these years of gathering sorrows, far
from renouncing his philosophical and religious
optimism, express it more forcibly than ever. In
1453, news of the taking of Constantinople by the
Turks was brought to him with the letter of Aeneas
Sylvius from which we have cited the mournful
phrases " Praecisus est fluvius omnium doctrinarum.
Musarum dessicatus est fons. Nunc Poesis, nunc
Philosophia sepulta videtur."[12] To Nicholas this
might have seemed even more the collapse of all his
youthful dreams.

But the winter of 1453-1454 saw the production of
his *De pace fidei* in spite of his isolation in his see of
Brixen and its atmosphere of hostility. This work is
perhaps more astonishing than all his others ; for
in spite of the agonizing prospect of a Moslem invasion of Europe, Nicholas did not recoil from
extending the bounds, already so ample, of his
Christian universalism. He proposed to the Turks
and to the pagans what is certainly the most generous
εἰρενιχὸν that had ever been conceived by a Catholic
theologian. The work was based on a study of
texts of the Koran which he had discovered during
his stay in Constantinople, among the Franciscans
of the Holy Cross, and which he had had explained
by them. Chimerical as his proposal may appear,
and as it in fact was, it was nevertheless a touching
attempt to elevate the Christian faith above everything that, as he put it, derived from a particular

12) " The flood of all knowledge has been stemmed. First poetry, then
philosophy seem to have been entombed."

civilization, and to prepare it for the most sweeping human changes.

But here again, and even more promptly than ever, his hopes for peace and unity were to lack foundation. In 1454, Nicholas had to assume the thankless task of attempting to assemble a Crusade at the Diet of Nuremburg. In 1460-1461, Pius II, in his turn, laboured in vain at Mantua on this same project. At this time while in Rome as the Pope's vicar Nicholas set himself to complete his *De pace fidei* by a *Cribratio Alchorani*. He attempted a systematic criticism of the insufficiencies of Islam as compared with Christianity. This he viewed, not as an abandonment, but rather a furthering of his aim for a rapprochment between the two cultures. Any effort in this direction, he felt, would be vain if it were not made with a perfect grasp of the factors involved. This explains the admirable letter which Pius II in his dying days wrote to Mohammed II under Nicholas' inspiration.

On August 11, 1464, Nicholas Krebs died prematurely, at work to the very end. Three days later, his friend the Pope followed him to the grave.

His noble figure stands between a world in collapse and a world being born. His splendid but unrealised " system " had doubtlessly attempted the impossible.

In spite of this, what commends him to us so highly is the Christian optimism with which in a thinker of such wonderful penetration we see the traditional faith confident, from the outset, in all that accrued from the Renaissance, even its most disconcerting elements. It was a confidence, we would say, in the ability of Catholicism to absorb every positive intellectual achievement of mankind ; a confidence, particularly, in the unlimited power of renewal and peaceful conquest peculiar to the Catholic faith itself.

CHAPTER VI

VITTORINO DA FELTRE

AFTER THE PRECURSOR of the Christian Renaissance, some account should be given of one of the most admirable of its initiators, the school-master of Mantua, Vittorino de Feltre. Vittorino de' Rambaldoni was born in 1378, some twenty years before Nicholas of Cusa, and died in 1446, a decade before him. But the nature of his work suggests that it be treated after that of Nicholas ; for since he deliberately limited himself to the work of education, it might be said that his principal achievement was the formation of certain of the most outstanding men of the next generation. [1]

Son of Bruto de' Rambadoni, a notary of Feltre, Vittorino was early put to his studies. He soon showed himself exceptionally gifted, and at the same time most devout, adopting a practice rare at the time of weekly Confession and of even more frequent Communion. He was never to abandon either and later recommended it constantly to his disciples. Nonetheless he appears to have been an extremely lively child, the leading spirit in games with other children. Although not well off, his parents managed to send him at an early age to the University of Padua. There he studied literature under the aegis of Conversino who had been a pupil of Petrarch's, and later under Barzizza, to whom Vittorino gives the credit for his own ex-

1) cf. Rosmini, *Vita e disciplina di V. da Feltre* (1801) and Woodward, *Vittorino da Feltre, Essays and Versions* (1897). There is also a small anonymous book in English, written by a religious, *Vittorino da Feltre, a Prince of Teachers* (London : 1908).

quisite Latin style. Finally, having gained his master of arts degree, he applied himself to mathematics, and even acted as servant to the famous Pelacano, so as to be able to pay the cost of his lessons.

His lack of money forced him while still studying to take on students of his own. A born teacher, he soon found himself at the head of a small group of disciples for whom he served as a spiritual father as well as school-master. It was at Padua also that Vittorino must have formed the habit he retained all his life of devoting a considerable part of the day, no matter how occupied with teaching or study, both to prayer and to visiting the sick in hospitals. Here, too, began his life-long friendship with many of his fellow pupils, among them the humanist Filelfo and in particular the great hellenist Guarino.

It was at the appeal of the latter that Vittorino, anxious to complete his own formation by the study of Greek, moved his private school to Venice where his friend was then established.

In 1420, after the Black Death had scattered his pupils, and Guarino had retired to his native city of Verona, Vittorino returned to Padua. There for two years more he taught Latin and mathematics at the university, before succeeding Barzizza in the chair of rhetoric. This masterful teaching, despite his great popularity, only lasted a year. Disgusted by the indiscipline of the students, and still more discouraged by his inability to exert any personal influence on the unruly mob, he set out again for Venice. He re-opened a school there and had considerable success. But this new stay likewise proved of brief duration. In the autumn of 1423 Vittorino set out again, this time for Mantua. On the recommendation of Guarino, Prince Giovanni

Francesco of Gonzaga had summoned him to become tutor to his children. It was here, then, that his life's work really began. Vittorino now realised that, despite his learning, his vocation was rather to be an educator than university professor.

It was no easy task that was now entrusted to him. Luigi, the eldest son of the prince was no better than a great lout, coarsened by perpetual over-indulgence in delicacies, while the younger son, Carlo, was of a violent and quarrelsome character. But Vittorino was not the man to shirk difficulties. He had already insisted on one condition, that he was to have full freedom in his methods. For example, there was no question of a private education for the young princes ; and, in a house on the banks of the Mincio, belonging to the Gonzagas, Vittorino set up a real school on his own lines. Luigi, Carlo and their sister Margaret were educated there in the company of young nobles from the neighbourhood and of another group of students brought from Venice by their master. The whole group consisted of some fifty children.

In accordance with his practice at Venice, Vittorino began by looking carefully into the character of each of his pupils. Then he sent away all those who either would or could not submit to his requirements. He used the same discrimination in regard to all assigned to help him, even the servants. This sifting once completed, the life of the school began. Severe though Vittorino was in the essential points of his firm but supple method, the house very soon came to be known as the *Casa Gioiosa*. The Renaissance offers few examples of so original an accomplishment or of one so profoundly penetrated with the Christain spirit ; which is why this " House of Joy " deserves our attention.

F

The vast building, light and airy, which the
Gonzagas had placed at Vittorino's disposition
lent itself admirably to his plans. But he hastened
to fence in the surrounding woods and fields in the
midst of this Virgilian countryside, to prevent
curious visitors from mingling with his students.
It seems that in his eyes one of the primary elements
of education was the creation and maintenance
among his students of an atmosphere wholly derived
from him. This was his idea in having all the sump-
tuous furniture and tapestries removed from the
house. Taking advantage of the soft, though at
times invigorating Italian climate, he declared war
on luxury and comfort, going so far as to ban all
heating. On the other hand, he spared no effort
to give the house an atmosphere of light and grace,
by means of works of art capable of elevating and
forming the minds of his students. The predomin-
ating note he seemed to desire was one of joyful
austerity.

There were four distinguishing characteristics in
his pedagogical scheme. A very important feature
of his system was the collective nature of his education.
He did not hesitate to organize " mixed education "
to some extent. The young daughters of the Gonzagas,
such as the Princesses Marguerite and Cecilia,
took part in the lessons and the exercises of the
school. In general, the young princes had to mix
on the same level with their comrades, some of whom
were nobles, but many of whom were of very modest
origins, such as the children of Guarino and of
Filelfo. They all shared both in the morning and
afternoon classes, and in the physical exercises, in
which there was constant competition. One of the
points on which Vittorino showed himself inflexible
was that all had to play together.

This brings us to a second characteristic, perhaps the most strikingly original on Vittorino's part, particularly in relation to schooling in the Middle Ages. [2] Open-air games, and in general, bodily activity, which he wanted to be plentiful, varied and happy, formed an integral part of the education given at the Casa Gioiosa. Twice a day, at the end of the morning and of the afternoon, at least one hour was so spent. No one was dispensed, whatever the weather, and Vittorino was himself one of the leading spirits. In a letter of Platina, librarian to Pope Sixtus IV, we find that for Vittorino this was part of a humane education. It included knowing " how to jump, run, mount a horse, throw the javelin, handle a sword, draw the bow." [3] Equally considerable was the attention he devoted to the formation of good manners, and he came to give more and more time to education in art. Many artists such as Primatice came from his school. It even became a centre of the most varied arts. He had, especially, a very high opinion of the value of music in education. The house was certainly joyful, with its continual sound of musical instruments and young voices.

In the third place, Vittorino expressly considered classical education, even in its narrowest sense, as the means to the formation of the whole man. Consequently he rejected all the futile subtleties of moribund scholasticism and stressed the importance of individual practice in correct diction and literary composition, with which the evenings were occupied. Above all, this formation, which drew on the whole of the ancient culture he was himself so

2)   cf.   also Erasmus' remarks based on experience in reference to Standonck in his *Colloquy On Eating Fish.*

3)   Cited in Morçay, *La Renaissance* (Paris : n.d.), I. p. 229.

thoroughly versed in, was always kept subservient and orientated to the Christian spirit. Although a layman, Vittorino recited the breviary every day, and gave personally the religious instruction as well as the secular. His students went with him to Mass every morning, and afterwards recited the Office of Our Lady.

Finally, he attached great importance in education to personal influence. For him there was no such thing as education apart from this. Hence he would not accept children whom he could not get to know intimately and become familiar with. Though exacting strictly a certain minimum of discipline and work, he made every effort to be a friend and confidant of his pupils. He joined in their games even when quite advanced in age, and shared all their youthful interests. He knew how to make himself respected, while encouraging an open and unconstrained relationship by keeping in close and affectionate contact with his pupils. In fact he seems to have had an altogether exceptional influence in the spiritual sphere.

Through the children he reached the parents, particularly in the case of the Gonzagas, Prince Giovanni Francesco and his wife, Paola de Malatesta. But here again it was one of Vittorino's firm principles that education could only be fully effective if begun in the very first years of childhood, a period hitherto completely neglected. His most remarkable successes among the Gonzagas were with Gian Lucido, confided to his care at the age of three, and particularly with Cecilia and Alexander, whom he looked after almost from their birth.

The depth of this influence is explained in part by the fact that it was continuous. Holidays, as we know them, hardly existed in the 15th century.

Nevertheless, during the warm season, the fear of malaria caused the transference of this ' School of Joy ' to the Alpine residence of the Gonzagas at Goito. Life there was freer than at Mantua and frequent excursions broke up the study periods. But Vittorino did not relax his attention to his pupils. He joined in their amusements and led their ramblings during the beautiful summer days. One excursion would take them to a nearby monastery of the Camaldolese monks, where the humanist Ambrogio Traversari was prior. On foot or horseback or by boat, master and pupils would go down along the Mincio as far as Lake Garda.

This constant hourly contact with the children, with the incessant calling into play of all the various qualities of the educator, demanded a personality richly and highly talented. Consequently, Vittorino continued his own personal studies even in the stress of his educational work and at the same time lived, though a layman, the interior life of a priest or religious.

On several occasions, Pope Eugene IV told people able to profit by it that they had in this man a real example of sanctity. But the secret of his art lay, no doubt, in the gracious fashion in which he presented in such an attractive light, to those entrusted to him, his Christian ideal in his own cultural setting.

CHAPTER VII

PICO DELLA MIRANDOLA

IT WOULD BE interesting to study in the lives of a number of pupils of Vittorino da Feltre the new type of christian his pedagogical methods had produced, as well as the new christian attitude to life and the world which was theirs. But none of them so well represents the christian temper in the first generations of the fully developed Renaissance as the precocious genius of whom we have now to speak. No one of that generation rivalled Pico della Mirandola, so brilliantly endowed, in the boldness of his effort to make a christian synthesis of the intellectual products of the Renaissance.

Born in 1463, in the castle of Mirandola, not far from Mantua, he died in Florence on the 17th of November, 1494, the very day that Charles VIII made his solemn entrance into the town. Giovanni Pico seems to us, in the phrase of Walter Pater, the prince charming of the Renaissance. [1]

After studying canon law at Bologna, and Greek at Ferrara under Giovanni Batista, the son of Guarino, Pico became first the pupil, then the friend of Ermolao Barbaro at Padua. It was this master who started him on the study of Aristotle, which he was then bringing up to date by the application of humanistic methods.

1) cf. the clear, conscientious exposition of M. Gautier Vignal, *Pic de la Mirandole* (Paris : 1937), which although well documented is really only a popularization. Several important studies have come out in Italy, recently : Semprini, *La Filosofia di Pico* (Milan : 1936); Agnanine, *Giovanni Pico della Mirandola, Sincretismo religioso-filosofico* (Bari : 1937); and particularly the fine work of Garino, *Giovanni Pico della Mirandola, Vita e dottrina* (Florence : 1947).

After two years, the war forced Pico to leave
Padua and retire to a villa he had built for himself
near Mirandola. There he gathered a number of
learned men also cast adrift by the events of the
time. Among them was Aldus Manitius who was
soon to become one of the most famous printers
in all Europe. In this retreat, Pico devoted himself
to the study of Greek, under the guidance of the
Cretan Adramitteno, and to Hebrew—which he
had started at Padua—under the direction of the
Jew, Elias of Medigo, who had followed him into
retirement. While staying there he also made the
acquaintance of Savonarola at Reggio. The same
year, or the following one, we find him corresponding
with two Florentines : Marsiglio Ficino, of whom he
requested a copy of his *Theologia platonica* which
was in preparation, and the poet Angelo Poliziano,
to whom the young count of Mirandola submitted
his own Latin and Italian verses.

But the differences then existing between his
two elder brothers, Galeotto and Antonio Maria,
obliged him to leave Mirandola. He went to the
university of Pavia for a few months. After another
equally short stay, this time with his sister, the
princess of Carpi, probably in the summer of 1484,
he went up to Florence attracted by the platonic
academy and the whole intellectual atmosphere that
surrounded Lorenzo the Magnificent. In this " City
of the Red Lily " he spent the most splendid year
of his short life, a close friend of Lorenzo the Magnificent, Marsiglio Ficino and Poliziano. Florence
was at the height of its glory both in art and literature. At the finest moment of Italian civilization,
sharing the intellectual enthusiasm of his young
companions, Pico della Mirandola was himself at
the most brilliant phase of his own youth. In his

preface to a translation of Plotinus dedicated to
Lorenzo, Ficino has described—no doubt with a
certain poetic licence—the dazzling appearance of
this fair and beautiful youth with his angelic countenance, at work in his darkened chamber where a
lamp burned perpetually before a bust of Plato.
We have a further witness to these friendships of
Pico's, and to the admiration which he commanded
in Florence, in a fresco painted in 1488 by Cosimo
Reselli in the church of St. Ambrose where he can
be recognized directly between Ficino and Poliziano.

This was the year in which the young count
seems to have conceived the project of a reconciliation of both platonism and aristotelianism with
traditional christian theology. Thus we see him
enriching his early aristotelian training at Padua
with his new, recent discovery of Plato while at
Florence. At the same time, he showed the same
concern for an eirenic christian intellectual attitude
as had Nicholas of Cusa. It remained to the end
the philosophical ideal of the Christians of the
Renaissance.

The real originality of Pico della Mirandola, in
face of the growing contempt of his time for the
Middle Ages, lay in his fidelity to the masters of
scholasticism, and especially to St. Thomas Aquinas.
It was precisely at this moment that he affirmed his
resolution to keep intact their heritage in the new
synthesis it was his ambition to produce. A long
letter, of April, 1485, gives an account of his intention
to the aristotelian Ermolao Barbaro. We see him
fully aware of the astonishment caused by his views
to all around him, but ready to defend them vigorously. His attachment to the scholastics caused
him to make a journey to Paris in July of 1485 and
to reside in the Latin quarter until April of 1486, in

order to perfect his understanding of their system
and methods.   It was here that his project must
have taken its final form.   He decided to hold a
public disputation, in which he would defend
against any opponent a whole body of theses making
up a truly encyclopedic *summa*.

On his return he passed through Florence without
staying.   He could not find there the quietness
necessary for his work.   Besides, it was at Rome
itself that he wanted to carry on the great intellectual contest of which he was so enamoured.   In
the course of his journey there he experienced in
the small town of Arezzo a sentimental adventure
quite in the manner of the *Decameron*.   Indeed
until then the nobility of his character and the
sublime nature of his intellectual activities had not
prevented the youthful prince leading a life highly
charged with emotion.   There is more than one
trace in the poems which he did not destroy.   But
this episode in which a number of his servants were
killed and he himself left wounded on the ground
seems to have quickly sobered him.   In any case,
his contemporaries are agreed upon his serious manner
of life from this time on.   Soon, under the influence
of Savonarola, the " prince charming " would even
be thinking of the monastic life, and he was to die
in the Dominican habit a few years later.

In any case it was while he was convalescing and
finishing his dissertations first at Perugia, then at
Fratta whither the plague had banished him, that
he made the last of his discoveries, in the autumn
of 1486.   A letter to Marsiglio Ficino, written at
this time, tells us that he was applying his whole mind
to Arabic and Chaldean (we would say Aramaic),
with a view to studying the extraordinary books
which he had just come upon.   These books were

the Cabala, which he was to introduce to the intellectual and learned circles of the day. The works
of Gershom Sholem have finally solved the mystery
of this Judaic gnosis.[2] Its source and even date
were still uncertain in the sixteenth century and were
the subject of fabled accounts. Through the inter-
mediary of Pico and then of his friend, the Hebrew
scholar Reuchlin, it was to become well established
in the humanist philosophy. Subsequently it seems
to have had a widespread influence on the whole
intellectual development of modern literature, as
shown by recent studies, such as those of Denis
Saurat.[3]

From the vast assemblage of ideas worked out
by this young man in his dashing way, there finally
emerged 900 theses. They were printed in Rome
in November 1486 under the title : *Conclusiones
nongentae in omni genere scientiarum.*[4] These theses
together with the *Discourse on the Dignity of Man*
which Pico had also prepared, doubtless to introduce their public discussion, may be considered
his principal work.

Of the 900 theses, 402 attempted to comprise all
theological and philosophical opinions, 115 of them
being devoted to scholasticism, from St. Albert
the Great to Giles of Rome, 82 to the Arabian
commentators on Aristotle, 29 to the ancient Greek
peripatetic philosophers, 99 to the neo-Platonists,
14 to the " mathematics of Pythagoras," that is to
speculations on numbers, six to the opinions of the
" Chaldean Theologians " meaning astrology, ten
to the " doctrine of Mercury Trismegistus," meaning
the *Poimandres* to which Ficino attached such

2) *Major Trends in Jewish Mysticism* (New York : 1946), pp. 156 ff.
3) *La littérature et l'occultisme* (Paris : 1929).
4) The title *De omni re scibili*—" On everything knowable "—is a quip
of Voltaire's.

great importance, and finally 47 to the Cabala. The 498 others expound Pico's own personal ideas.

His *Discourse on the Dignity of Man*[5] well summarises the scope of this formidable compilation. The whole first part (the only section that really corresponds to the title) is, as it were, the spiritual manifesto of the Renaissance.[6] Pico begins by exalting man, as a being whose consciousness of an inherent nobility should be a constant incentive to perfection in every way possible. This exordium is clearly stamped with Ficino's neo-Platonism. What follows is more original. He justifies his passion for philosophy and his universal curiosity as the means he desires to use for his own response to man's vocation so conceived. He is thereby led to the idea which is the first basis of his whole system. This he owes to the neo-Platonists whom he combines with the Christian writers of Alexandria : in the esoteric meaning of the ancient philosophers or religions, there is, according to him, a latent confirmation of the truths of Christianity. Thence he goes over to the eclecticism—it would be better perhaps to call it syncretism—which is the foundation of his thought. He justifies it by the need to gather into the one truth its fragments lying scattered in various places. Finally, there is an essay in defence of the strangest parts of his work, those dealing with the doctrine of numbers, with occultism, and specially with the Cabala.

From all this, and in the theses themselves, one gets the impression of the greatest effort at concordism

5)   Edited by E. Garino (Florence : 1942).

6)   Walter Pater is opposed to this idea in *The Renaissance* (London : 1873, new ed. 1935), p. 37. He sees here no more than a survival of medieval anthropomorphism. This is surprising coming from so fine a critic. For the opposite view, see Burckhardt, *Civilization of the Renaissance in Italy* and the remarks of Imbart de la Tour, *Les origines de la Reforme*, vol. II (Paris : 1909), pp. 323 to 330.

ever attempted by a Christian thinker. One of Pico's titles was Prince of Concordia, and it is understandable that he took pride in it, He had the same ambition to achieve a universal, intellectual reconciliation under the aegis of Catholicism as had Nicholas of Cusa. But the resemblance in their deepest desires was less marked than their differences. The mind of the one was fuller of hope than of attainments. In the other, we are bewildered by the profusion of his knowledge. But compared with the monolithic synthesis achieved by the first, the constructional weakness of the second is lamentable. In Nicholas of Cusa we see an intellectual effort highly concentrated and powerful, attempting to harmonise from the outset within the Catholic faith all the various conclusions to which science was still feeling its way. In the case of Pico, on the contrary, the new knowledge has been surveyed in every direction. His aim, furthermore, is precisely to preserve the principles of the traditional scholasticism while expanding and developing it according to the new discoveries. But his synthesis has a want of firmness and vagueness that shows his thought is as yet immature. He is only too obviously dazzled by his wealth of ideas, and is overwhelmed by them.

The story of the condemnation of thirteen of the nine hundred theses, after Pope Innocent VIII had forbidden them to be defended in public debate, and of the brief of August 4, 1487, ordering that the copies of the whole should be burnt, need not be related here. In any case it raises more than one historical problem not yet resolved, particularly that of whether the *Apology* composed by Pico immediately after his submission to the condemnation of the theses, was published before or after the brief. This latter document affirmed : " We declare however that the Count of Mirandola's good name remains unsullied since he has only proposed and published these theses in preparation for a scholastic discussion and under the control of the Holy See ; and that he himself has declared that he holds them only as we judge them, and that he has taken an oath never to defend them again."[7]

As a matter of fact, Pico's *Apology* does make an attempt to defend them, in disclaiming the interpretations, alleged by him to be calumnious, which caused them to be condemned. Consequently, though he does indeed finish by renewing the act of his submission to the sovereign pontiff, the latter had him arraigned for perjury and rebellion and sought out in France where he had taken refuge. Pico underwent a brief imprisonment, actually quite comfortable in the chateau of Vincennes. He was freed by the intervention of Lorenzo de Medici ; but it was only under Alexander VI that he would once more enjoy the favour of the Holy See.

Until the death of Lorenzo, he resided in the neighbourhood of Florence, at Fiesole, or in Florence itself. He continued his studies and his publications. Most characteristic of this period is a commentary of his on the *Canzone* of Benivieni on platonic love, defined as the attraction of the Beautiful. After the death of Lorenzo, in 1492, he retired to Ferrara, where he lived in solitude, never showing himself at court, completely absorbed in his religious concerns. In this year he wrote to his nephew Giovanni Francesco the letter *De contemptu mundi*, which a little later was to delight St. Thomas More. When Innocent VIII died, Pico returned to Florence, intending it only as a stage on the road to Rome.

7) Cited by L. Gautier in *Pic de La Mirandole*, p. 134.

There he received on June 18, 1493, the letter of
Alexander VI absolving him from all censure. The
preaching of Savonarola and the two men's friendship prevented him, however, from going farther.

Like so many others of this period, this young
philosopher, intoxicated by the world and its splendor, passionately desirous of reconciling all of it
within Christianity, was to pass swiftly to the
opposite extreme of an almost inhuman religion.
Did he sense the coming of death which could hardly
have been expected ? He disposed of almost all
his possessions, and, an indefatigable reader, con-
tented himself with reading nothing else than St.
Paul. The preparation of his final work, *Against
Astrology*, seems to have been his only reason for
delay in joining the Dominicans. His trials increased,
first Lorenzo died, then Ermolao Barbaro, then
Poliziano. Soon he joined the latter, being buried
next to him in the church of St. Mark. He died, as
we have said, the day of the French invasion, no
doubt poisoned by his servants for the sake of money.

CHAPTER VIII

ERASMUS, MORE AND *THE PRAISE OF FOLLY*

WITH ERASMUS WE reach the maturity of the entirely new type of Christian personality and thought that we have seen in preparation under teachers such as Vittorino da Feltre, and flowering in that youthful prodigy, Pico della Mirandola. [1] Erasmus was only three years younger than Pico, but his career continued until 1536, and humanist theology, in the sense in which we understand it here, was able, in his hands, to cast off the impetuosity and exuberance of youth. It is noteworthy that a man from the Low Countries was unquestionably the chief representative of this phase of humanism. With the end of the fifteenth century Italian humanism may be said to have ended. Its development seems to have been arrested. After a period of quiet, which might give an illusion of stability, though decay could already be detected, it withered and straightway collapsed. [2]

1) The literature on Erasmus is immense and we cannot pretend to give even a summary bibliography. Besides the recent studies of M. Renaudet, the examination of which will form the core of our work, we will only cite, among the French publications of these last years, the work of M. J. B. Pineau, *Erasme, sa pensée religieuse* (Paris : 1924) and M. Gautier-Vignal, *Erasme* (Paris : 1936). The latter has the same qualities as the author's book on Pico. The great work for a total view is still James A. Froude, *The Life and Letters of Erasmus*, (London : 1894). For his youth, there is that considerable work, Seebohm, *The Oxford Reformers : John Colet, Erasmus* and *Thomas More*, (London : 1887), which is extremely narrow in its judgements but rich in facts and citations. However, these works have been superceded by a monumental publication : P. S. and H. M. Allen, *Opus epistolarum Des. Erasmi Roterodami denuo recognitum et auctum* (Oxford : 1906-47 11 vols). The only complete biography is that of Huizinga, *Erasme*, French edition (Paris : 1955). For the rest of Erasmus' works, the better edition is still that of Le Clerc in eleven folio volumes (Leyden : 1703-1706).

2) cf. Imbort la Tour, *op. cit.*, vol. II, pp. 344-345.

We do not propose to sketch, even in outline, the life of Erasmus. We shall just recall the principal stages of a career so fertile in results. After studying at Deventer, then at Bois-le-Duc, he spent some years in the monastery at Steyn, in the course of which his true vocation became clear. When in 1492 he left the monastery, never to return, he was already in correspondence with many of the humanists, and carried away with him his first two works : the *Contempt of the World* and *The Book of Anti-Barbarians*.

Then began the years of what may be called his apprenticeship, years that were often difficult, when he was on the move between Paris and the Low Countries. His good fortune began in 1499 with his first journey to England, thanks to his student and friend, Lord Mountjoy. There he met More, became the friend of Colet, and was presented to the future King Henry VIII. On his return to Paris he brought out the first edition of his *Adages* and a little while later, his *Enchiridion militis christiani*. He studied Greek and published Valla's *Annotations* on the New Testament.

Erasmus made a number of journeys to Holland, Artois, Louvain, Paris and once again to England. In 1506 he started out for Italy. There he resided in each of the principal intellectual centres in turn, and particularly in Venice with Aldus Manutius, who brought out the great edition of the *Adages*. There followed a stay in Rome. In 1509, the coronation of Henry VIII brought him to England. It was then that he became the guest and the intimate friend of Thomas More. On his return to Paris, Erasmus published his *The Praise of Folly* and almost immediately returned to England where he stayed some time. These comings and goings were repeated frequently. In between times he visited Flanders once more, then Alsace and Basel. He published his *Novum Instrumentum* (the New Testament in Greek), his edition of St. Jerome, the *Instruction for a Christian Prince*, and the *Querimonia Pacis*. In these years he was at the height of his fame.

From 1517 to 1521 his attention was mainly occupied by the commencement of what was to be known as the Reformation, and at the same time he published his *Paraphrases on the Epistles*. In 1521, his too conciliatory attitude toward the Lutherans made it impossible for him to stay longer in Louvain, although he had almost settled there since Charles V had made him a counsellor of the Empire. It was then that he decided to establish himself in Basel. 1521 to 1529 were those extremely productive years of which Renaudet has made a special study and on which we will dwell later.

Here we just note that at this time Erasmus published the *Paraphrases on the Gospels*, the *Colloquies* (in a new form, making it a sort of breviary of all his ideas), *De Libero Arbitrio*, and the *Ciceronianus*. It was, too, his most productive period as editor of the writers of the ancient world. But in 1529 there occured an event corresponding to that which had made him leave Louvain in 1521. Refusing to compromise with the Reformation as he had earlier refused to condemn it in principle, he had to leave Basel as he had had to flee Louvain.

During his last years, while in Fribourg, he published the treatise *For the Reestablishment of Concord in the Church*. In 1535, he started north hoping either to reach the Low Countries, or to set himself up at Besançon. But he was obliged by sickness to stop at Basel with Jerome Frobenius. There this ceaseless traveller died, during the night of July 11

G

to July 12, 1536, soon after publishing his *Ecclesiastes*, an essay on the method of preaching.

Since we are concerned not with a study of the enormous output of Erasmus, but with an understanding of his spirit and general trend, the years at Basel—when ' Erasmianism ' showed itself clearly as lying between an ultra-conservative Catholicism and the Protestant innovators—are the really significant ones. The close scrutiny to which Renaudet has subjected them in his *Etudes érasmiennes*, together with the synthesis he has formed so judiciously, make him the obvious guide to follow ; though we reserve the right to criticise him after he has introduced us to the heart of the problems involved. But we must, first of all, dispose of the one question which stands in the way of anyone desirous of interpreting the work and the thought of Erasmus, and that will complete our introduction to the finest example of humanist theology.

The problem is that raised by Erasmus' *The Praise of Folly*. The great majority of authors who have spoken of Erasmus seem for the most part to have read nothing else of his than this slight volume, or else to have read (or perused) the rest of his works in the light of this lively but sibylline pamphlet. In addition, the most surprising errors are often committed by not paying attention to the literary genre which it represents. This results in interpretations which, seemingly literal, are yet completely misleading. These have to be weeded out ; for, if they were admitted, there would be no point in proceeding further. It would be as profitable to examine the theology of Lucan or of Voltaire, as to attempt to elucidate that of Erasmus.

At first sight, indeed *The Praise of Folly* might pass for an extravagant mockery of Catholic theology

or the Church itself, not to speak of other institutions
whose connection with the latter made them all a
part of what was still called Christendom.

But first it must be said that the literary genre of
The Praise of Folly is of its very nature highly misleading. It is akin to those verbal pleasantries
which grow and expand in a small select group,
and then, one fine day, are given shape and published to the outside world. They begin as a game,
the kind of thing indulged in by a group of students
or artists. In becoming the object of continual
allusions, apparently in all seriousness to those
outside the group, but to the initiate merely flippant,
the game is completely baffling to one who only
reads about it. And no key can ever quite give the
exact meaning of the text in question. To understand it, and particularly to judge of its importance,
one must have been a participant in the common
elaboration of the burlesque. In other words,
publication of this kind of thing inevitably leads to
misunderstanding ; it is a psychological error.
If it interests anyone outside the group, it is only
because he is one of the targets of abuse, and such
are not likely to learn from it. That is the case with
the *Encomium Moriae*.

Written down in one sitting by Erasmus, after a
long and intimate talk with Thomas More, it is
strongly redolent of that atmosphere *sui generis*
which this very unusual saint always produced.
In all justice to Erasmus it must be said that he did
everything to warn the reader, beginning with a
pun in the very title : *Encomium Moriae*. (The
Praise of Folly . . . or of More.)

There are few men in all English history of whom
humour is so characteristic as Thomas More. It
is a quality almost incomprehensible to the Latin

or the German. It belongs to the mind which loves
to utter fantastic statements with complete imper-
turbability, but implying thereby, though in extremely
paradoxical fashion, all sorts of commonsense
truths. That was the very spirit of Thomas More.
It is also precisely the spirit of *The Praise of Folly ;*
only that this has the inevitable drawback that parts
of it cannot possibly be grasped by the uninitiated
however intelligent, without becoming more or
less falsified in the process.

It goes without saying then that this little book
can only be understood in relation to the personality
and works of More. Erasmus insisted on this continually, but unfortunately, practically no one has
ever attempted it. There is not a single work of
More's, whether of religious controversy, or even
of edification, however serious, which does not contain page after page written in the same vein as
the Praise of Folly. On the other hand Erasmus
never tried his hand again at that sort of thing. We
will shortly see how different is the style of the
Colloquies, which are certainly the work of Eramsus.
Consequently, we are bound to attribute the *Folly*
to a wholesale appropriation or, perhaps, a momentary intoxication of Erasmus by More's humour.

The calmness and remorseless logic with which
the most outrageous explanations of human life,
and particularly of religion, are upheld in the book
must not mislead us. This pseudo-nihilism is perfectly compatible with a robust faith. In fact, he is
simply laughing at humbug, that is at people who
confuse their personal insignificance with the importance of their function.

Such an interpretation is clearly indicated when
we look at the *Folly* in conjuction with another
cast of mind, prevalent in the Middle Ages, and

more particularly in mediaeval Germany, whence came the humanism of Erasmus.

If there is one traditional theme not only in our fables, but especially in those basically religious productions such as the *danses macabres* of the fifteenth century,[3] it is the pretended damnation of popes, princes and monks. To attribute to these satires a tendency analogous to our modern anti-clericalism is to forget that those who perpetrated these things were more often than not the very persons who were being ridiculed. (In our own day, perhaps the most pungent stories about the clergy are those current among the clergy themselves).

We should, then, be in no hurry to see in the *Encomium* an attack on the papacy, or its ally the civil power, still less a bomb hurled at the Church ; nor should we forget that Erasmus was a coun-sellor of the Empire, as well as a priest. It is simply a bitter satire against the identification by med-iocre individuals of themselves and the causes they claim to be serving. Actually these causes come out quite unharmed inasmuch as they are never touched upon in the whole work. This is what Erasmus always asserted. Hence nothing justifies the attribution to him by the great majority of historians of a Machiavellian plan, the opposite of what he professed. All becomes clear if the *En-comium* is viewed in its proper setting and compared to other pieces of its kind. As he himself has said, the *Encomium* only took on a different meaning when long after its composition and publication, this satire on persons was gratuitously interpreted as a satire on institutions. The blame for this rests on Hutten and Luther. The prudence, or otherwise, of publishing such an enigmatic work is a totally

3)   cf. Emile Male, *Histoire de l'art du Moyen Age*, vol. III (Paris : 1932).

different matter. But again it must be remembered that in 1515 it was difficult to foresee what the heretics, who were at that time still considered irreproachable Catholics, would make of it ten years later.

One thing is certain, and it is all that concerns us here, namely, that *The Praise of Folly* must be allowed the same latitude that all competent historians today grant to More's *Utopia*. Both are deliberately paradoxical works written in leisure moments, and in such cases the most literal interpretations are the most fallacious. All the more reason then, for not allowing such works—mere youthful amusements—to influence our judgement of other far more extensive ones, written in extremely critical circumstances. Written as it was in a light-hearted frame of mind when there was nothing serious to engage the attention, the book must not be allowed to influence our study of the longer works written at the height of the storm, and still less be held to dispense us from it. The way is now clear for the work in hand.

BOOK III

THE ERASMIAN STUDIES OF AUGUSTIN RENAUDET

AND

THE TRUE INTERPRETATION OF ERASMUS

OUR ATTENTION WILL first of all be directed to an analysis and criticism of a work of capital importance in the study of the Renaissance. This is true particularly of our own standpoint which concerns humanist Christian thought, the clarification of the idea itself, and the history of its development.

We refer to the volume *Etudes érasmiennes 1521-1529*, by Augustin Renaudet, professor at the Sorbonne, published in 1939 in Paris by Droz.

The importance of this work stems first of all from the reputation of its author. M. Renaudet is one of the most eminent historians of the sixteenth century. Well known especially for his book *Préréforme et humanisme à Paris pendant les premières guerres d'Italie* (1494-1517), M. Renaudet has devoted himself above all to the study of Erasmus. Already, in 1913, he published a book on *Erasme, sa vie et son œuvre jusqu'en 1517, d'après sa correspondance.*

We should perhaps note in passing the astonishment we felt in not finding any mention of this first book in those which have followed it. Could this be because the author has detached himself from the production of his youth, to which nevertheless his later works are so closely related ? Whatever the explanation, in 1926 M. Renaudet brought out another volume called : *Erasmus, his religious thought and activity according to his correspondence* (1518-1521). This small volume gave evidence of the author's competence. It displayed considerable delicacy in approaching a problem posed by a writer who is among the most enigmatic in all literature : what was the position taken by Erasmus during the decisive years of Luther's evolution ? A third volume, giving evidence of progress in research and development over its predecessors, brings the same thinker's career up to the year 1529, when Erasmus was forced to leave Basel before the violent triumph of the Reformation.

But for these years which are capital for his subject, M. Renaudet is no longer content to continue exploiting the magnificent Oxford edition of the *Letters of Erasmus*. He now utilizes the material furnished by the *Letters* as a solid historical background to portray his analysis of the works that Erasmus composed and published during his stay in Basel.

M. Renaudet commences with a preparatory chapter entitled *Projets et Voyages*. Then, under the title *Science critique et dispute*, he presents a general review of Erasmus' biblical and patrological works, the compositions devoted to spirituality, the *Apologias* (addressed either to Catholics or to Lutherans), the humanist preoccupations, and finally the essays and polemical writings which Erasmus produced during this fruitful period of his life.

The reader is thus treated to a detailed examination of a) " The Erasmian Criticism of Government and of Society " (chapter 3); b) what M. Renaudet calls " Erasmian Modernism " (chapter 4); c) " Erasmus and the Catholic Church " (chapters 5 and 6); and finally, " Erasmus and the Reformation " (chapters 7 and 8).

In a long and very enlightening Introduction, M. Renaudet excuses himself for not attempting an exhaustive study of either the thought or the personality of Erasmus, by relating one or the other of these aspects of his subject to the period he has in mind. His only hope, he assures us, is to present a series of converging monographs on certain particularly important aspects of Erasmus' intellectual position. It is precisely this position, so difficult to characterize, that has been the permanent concern of M. Renaudet in the course of all the works that he has consecrated to Erasmus. It is this feature that occupies his attention so particularly in the four hundred or so pages of his last volume. In this regard, the chapter entitled " Erasmian Modernism " constitutes the very heart of the work. It is naturally to this chapter that our attention and our criticism will be directed. But first we must trace the career of Erasmus in the company of M. Renaudet.

CHAPTER IX

THE CRUCIAL YEARS IN THE LIFE OF ERASMUS

AFTER HE HAD left Louvain on October 28, 1521, when his situation had become impossible, Erasmus reached Basel on November 15. He had no intention of residing there. The fact is that with the winter hardly ended, he had made up his mind to return to the north. But his poor health kept him at Selestat. When he learned that Charles V was no longer in the Low Countries, Erasmus gave up the journey, and came back to Basel. He did not propose to remain there, however, any longer than would be necessary to finish certain works destined for Froben, from now on his official publisher.

He was expected in Rome, where leisure for study and a friendly society would have greatly delighted him, only that he feared being forced to throw himself into the battle against Luther. He knew that, since he had been reproached for his tolerance in regard to Luther in Louvain, in Rome he would be expected to come out against the reformer by engaging in a polemic obviously distasteful to him. He was also wanted in Paris, as Bude had written to him in this vein in 1517 ; and Zwingli tried to make him come to Zurich. This last invitation, however, Erasmus had courteously but categorically refused !¹

Finally he decided to go to Rome. But sickness again held him up in Constance. And on his recovery, he returned to Basel where he was once

1) Augustin Renaudet, *Etudes érasmiennes* 1521-1529 (Paris : 1939), p. 7.

more absorbed in his literary occupations. A letter
from the new pope, Adrian VI, another from Bude
with a post-script in the hand of King Francis
I, drew him in opposite directions. On top of this,
a direct effort was made to entice him to Wittemberg.
But to this overture his refusal was again unconditional. Then finally he made up his mind to
write against Luther. His *De libero arbitrio* appeared
in the autumn of 1524.

There was now nothing to prevent him falling in
with the wishes of Pope Adrian VI, since he had
given up his position as counsellor of the Emperor
at the instance of France. It is true that Marguerite
of Austria summoned him to the Low Countries,
but this prospect had little attraction for Erasmus.
Instead he set about putting himself on the road
to Rome, when in the early part of 1524 he suddenly
discovered that his opponent, the nuncio Alexander,
was about to arrive there. This news put an end
to any further preparations for departure. In the
course of his self-imposed solitude in Basel, Erasmus
distracted himself with a short journey to Besançon,
where even a most flattering reception could not
detain him. On several occasions he thought of
France, once more banking on an eventual reconciliation between king and emperor. But his cus-
tomary perspicacity in politics enabled him to forsee
the French collapse. The following year, he determined upon residence in Pavia.

Meanwhile life in Basel grew less bearable the
more the city came under the influence of the Reformation. In December, 1525, the appearance of
Luther's *De servo arbitrio* forced him to take sides
with the Catholic anti-Lutheran party. On all
sides he was deluged with offers from this camp :
from Poland, from Austria, from England, from

Spain ; but Rome alone was still capable of tempting
him. Yet the work which ceaselessly poured from
his pen kept him stationary at Basel. [2]

The end of 1527, however, which witnessed the
death of Froben, destroyed his last link with this
town now completely estranged from him. If he
rejected all that France offered at this time, it was
only because England called him with renewed
insistence. But Erasmus already scented difficulties
about to arise over the divorce of Henry VIII.

Finally he resigned himself to the idea of returning
to the Low Countries, thinking no doubt of Antwerp,
which had always held some attraction for him.
He was still hesitating however. At last an invitation
from the chancellor of Austria — the prince bishop
of Trent—reached him. This was highly gratifying,
particularly since it contained a prospect of settling,
not indeed in Vienna itself, but at Freiburg-im-
Breisgau. He prepared to leave at Easter ; but his
inevitable cold delayed him. Finally, on April 13,
1529, at mid-day, with no regret, he set out on the
Rhine, from near the Church of St. Anthony. His
first letter from Freiburg is dated April 21. His
stay in Basel, always on the point of ending, had
lasted eight years, and had produced the greater
part of his writings.

*   *   *

The second chapter of M. Renaudet's book
contains an inventory of the works of Erasmus
written during his years at Basel. They must be
mentioned briefly.

In March of 1519, Froben had issued a second

2) Renaudet, *op. cit.* p. 15. All further references giving page numbers
only are to this work.

edition of Erasmus' *Greek New Testament*, with a Latin translation by Erasmus himself. The first edition had appeared in 1516. Erasmus announced his translation of the Καινὴ διαθήκη by giving it the title *Novum instrumentum*. Contrariwise, in the translation of the text, M. Renaudet says Erasmus took great and unheard of liberties—rendering, for example, the *logos* in St. John's Gospel not by *verbum* but by *sermo*. But in February, 1522, in the third edition, he was more prudent. In deference to the criticism of Aleander and others, he put back the *comma johanneum*. He also omitted the introduction on method, but brought it out separately under the title of *Ratio verae theologiae*.[3] In 1527 there was a fourth edition, even more moderate in tone ; for the first time, giving way to his opponents, Erasmus combined the Vulgate with his own Latin version.

In his edition, Erasmus was not content merely to accompany the text with learned notes, but he wrote paraphrases in clear and flowing Latin anyone could understand. Before coming to Basel, he had written a commentary on the Epistles (republished in 1523 and 1524). Now he turned to the Gospels. In 1522 appeared his paraphrase of St. Matthew dedicated to Charles V. In 1523, those on St. John and St. Luke ; and in the spring of 1524 he brought out his St. Mark.

Erasmus was not a Hebrew scholar and had never been very much interested in the Old Testament, apart from Isaias and the Psalms. But now he prepared a commentary on Psalms II, III, IV, and V which appeared in 1528 in a form closer to the traditional type of commentary. M. Renaudet calls attention to the difference between these works,

3)   This had already been published separately in 1519.

addressed as they were if not to scholars at least to the learned—even if this were only by the Latin language in which they were written—and the Lutheran edition in the vernacular aimed at the masses.

It was during this same period, with the aid of a group of collaborators, that Erasmus was also busy bringing out editions of the Fathers of the Church— in 1520, 1521, 1525, of St. Cyprian ; in 1522, the *De Civitate Dei* of St. Augustine, with the enormous commentary of the erudite Juan Luis Vives. At the same time he produced, distinct from these, an *editio princeps* of Arnobius the Younger's commentary on the Psalms. In 1523 St. Hilary's works appeared. Erasmus, however, was more interested in the Greek Fathers. In 1523 he decided upon a complete edition of Origen and another of St. John Chrysostom. But as his publishers had their doubts about this, he first of all, between 1524 and 1526, re-edited carefully all the works of St. Jerome, his favourite among the Latin Fathers (he had already published an edition in 1516). All the same, in 1525, 1526, and 1527, Froben published various works of St. John Chrysostom ; in 1526, the *editio princeps* of Irenaeus ; in 1527, several treatises of St. Athanasius ; likewise in 1527, St. Ambrose, with several fragments of Origen on St. Matthew. Finally, in 1528-1529, there appeared the great edition of St. Augustine that had been so long awaited.

We pass now to his spiritual writings. In 1522 he had published his *De interdicto usu carnium*. It is actually a return to the doctrine of the *Enchiridion*, which appeared in 1594, on the opposition between the Gospel and the Jewish spirit, so attached to external practices as such. In 1523, he wrote, improbably enough, a Mass for pilgrims to Loreto—

to which he added a sermon in 1525. In 1523 again,
he composed a commentary on the Our Father,
which is his *Precatio Dominica in VII Partes* and
the following year a whole treatise on prayer, his
Modus orandi Deum. The same year, it seems,
there also came out his *Exomologesis,* or *De modo
confitendi* on Confession. In 1523, Erasmus had
written a short treatise for the Benedictines of Cologne on *Virginis et martyris comparatio.* In 1526
he dedicated to Catherine of Aragon his *Christiani
matrimoni institutio,* whose main ideas he reproduced in his *De vidua christiana,* addressed to Mary
of Hungary in 1529.

In the polemic field, as we have indicated, it was
only in 1524 that he brought out his *De libero
arbitrio* against Luther. Immediately after he thought
of writing a treatise on the Eucharist, but, in fact,
never did. As for personal *apologias,* particularly
in defense of his *New Testament,* he was obliged to
publish one against the Dutch Carmelite Nicholas
Baechem in 1522. The same year, he entered into
a courteous controversy with a professor of the
University of Alcala, Sanchez Carranza. And almost
at the same time, he launched two *apologias* in a
completely different spirit, against a colleague of
Carranza, Zuniga, who became one of his fiercest
adversaries. Zuniga profited by the death of Pope
Adrian VI to re-open the fight and Erasmus had
to reply to him again in 1524. In 1525, it was against
a Carthusian of Paris, Pierre Cousturier, the former
prior of the Sorbonne, that he had to defend himself. Then, in 1526 and 1527, he issued a number of
publications as a reply to Noel Beda, the syndic
of the Sorbonne, and to the condemnations passed
by this body on the rather tendentious translations
of his own works by Louis de Berquin. In the

H

beginning of 1528, he brought out the *Apologia ad monachos quosdam hispanos*. There are, besides, other works of minor importance.

During this same period, Erasmus was involved in disputes with the Lutherans. To the violent *Expostulatio* of Hutten, which had appeared in Strasbourg, in 1523, Erasmus replied with his *Spongia adversus aspersiones Hutteni*. In 1526 and 1527 he replied to Luther's *De servo arbitrio* which had been written in reply to his own *De libero arbitrio* with the two volumes of the *Hyperaspistes*. To these must be added the *Detectio prestigiarum etc.*, which came out also in 1526 in answer to an insidious and anonymous pamphlet, the work of a former follower of Erasmus from Alsace, now a pastor in Zurich, who attempted to twist his ideas about the Eucharist in a Lutheran sense.

It is obvious that his purely humanist work was restricted and badly hindered by this prodigious output of religious writings. All the same, even in these years, it did not altogether cease. In 1524, along with his edition of St. Augustine, he managed to bring out one of Cicero's Tusculan orations, though most of the work was done by his secretaries. In 1525, under similar conditions, were brought out the *Natural History* of Pliny and a number of treatises of Plutarch. In 1529, though he had small liking for stoicism, he brought out a masterly edition of Seneca.

It will suffice merely to mention the editions of his own *Colloquies*, which were enlarged with each new publication in 1522, 1523 and 1524. The same can be said of his *Adages*, appearing in 1520, 1523, 1526, and 1528. On the other hand, during his stay at Basel, Erasmus did not re-publish his *Praise of Folly*, for it had begun to cause scandal. But he allowed it to be reprinted at Mainz and in Cologne, at Strasbourg and Venice. Finally, in 1528, there appeared two connected works which are of special importance for the understanding of the development of Erasmian humanism ; *De recta latini graecique sermonos pronuntiatione*, and his *Ciceronianus*.

There is, too, his enormous correspondence which, prudently enough, he allowed to be published in small part only.

*   *   *

We now come to what constitutes the essence of Erasmus' work, as contained in the several titles under which M. Renaudet has grouped the chief parts. The problem dealing with Christian civilization is considered under the rubric *Critique of Government and of Society*. It is this concern with sociological matters that has led recent biographers of Erasmus[4] to yield to the temptation of concentrating on the most modern, but also most superficial side of his personality. This is the aspect, together with his constant travels, his familiarity with the great personages of the age, and his voluminous correspondence, in which he may be compared to Voltaire. Even so, comparison is misleading. At an any rate, his political interests were confined strictly to the circumstances of his own life, and of the relationships, epistolary and otherwise, it led to. M. Renaudet, in fact, shows that apart from some quite uncharacteristic passages in the works of his youth, this is a quite insignificant element in his writings. His criticisms of Lucian first of all, then of Plato's *Laws*, of the *Dream of Scipio*, and

---

4) cf. in particular, Stefan Zweig, *Erasme* (Paris : 1935) and Th. Quoniam, *Erasme* (Paris : 1935).

even of certain parts of Seneca less repugnant to him than the rest, all more or less contributed to the evangelical and Pauline frame of mind which made him say : *Ego mundi civis esse cupio.*[5]

Neither the historians nor the legal writers of antiquity interested him enough for him to learn much from them. The humanists themselves, till then, had written only in rhetorical vein. Machiavelli, it is true, had finished his *Prince* in December, 1513, but he was only slightly attracted to humanism. Erasmus did not know the work. As for the political doctrines of the Middle Ages, M. Renaudet assures us that Erasmus had no interest at all in them.

Contrary to what one would expect of a man engrossed in study, however, and more particularly when the object of his research is essentially literary, which means humane or more precisely psychological, Erasmus showed an insatiable curiosity for men and facts. And what is a rarity in a worker of his sort, he never excluded visitors, but he was always ready to receive practically anyone, never tired as long as he was brought some news. Add to this a gift for detailed observation, shown particularly in the pleasant anecdotes which make up his *Colloquies*, and often caused him to be compared to Lucian, a great object of his youthful admiration; bearing in mind too the extraordinary cosmopolitanism of his life making him intimate with several rulers and with innumerable statesmen such as Thomas More, we can then judge what account should be taken of his reflections and opinions on political matters. M. Renaudet notes a development both in his taste for such questions, and in the penetration of his remarks. Little on the subject appears in the first edition of his *Adages*

5) Allen, *op. cit.* vol. 5.

in 1500, but his interest in it is more pronounced in the Venetian edition of 1508, though still in the guise of literary reminiscences. But in 1511, when the *Encomium Moriae* appears in Paris, not only does it chastise severely the realist politics of Pope Julius II, but also contains some general observations on the incapacity of so many princes, and particularly on the absence among them and their entourages of all sense of their responsibilities.

The Basel edition of the *Adages*, resulting from experience gained by contact with the commercial bourgeoisie of the Low Countries, with the court of Henry VIII and with men such as Bude, More, and the German humanists, contains his first complete programme, political and religious. His commentary on such sayings as *Dulce bellum inexpertis ; Sileni Alcibiadis ;* and *Scarabeus aquilam quaerit*, reproduced and translated into modern language, read like manifestos. There he censures in exact detail the despotic character of the rulers of Europe of his time. He exposes in particular their exploitation of the state for their own pleasure and for that of their families. But what is perhaps the most striking of all is his unconditional condemnation of war, not indeed in the abstract (he reserves the theoretical possibility of a just war), but in the concrete. Giving a detailed analysis of the various pretexts habitually advanced in favour of warfare, he exposes the one reality hidden behind them all, or on the contrary revealed in all of them. It is either the vanity or the unrestrained ambition of princes.

By the same token, in his biblical commentaries, he uses hardly less severity in attacking the churchmen for deserting their domain, and even deliberately turning their backs on what is really the only reason for their existence. He maintains that far from seeking to appease national quarrels, or at least not allowing themselves to be mixed up in them, they fan the flames by applying religious sophisms or moral pretexts to wars kindled by pure unreflecting egoism.

M. Renaudet suggests a parallel between these ideas and certain notions of Dante in his *De Monarchia*. But he contrasts the Ghibelline ideas of Dante with the slight regard Erasmus had for an imperial supermonarch to be placed over all the national states. As a humanist, he saw therein only a new machine for imposing taxes, and believed rather in the efficacy of a federation of heads of states inspired by truly Christain ideals.

In connection with the favourable reception given these ideas by the great merchant bourgeoisie then arising, M. Renaudet makes a very interesting observation. Without condemning outright the taking of interest on capital that was simply invested in a business in which one took no further part, Erasmus saw clearly the tremendous social change it would effect. The enrichment of middlemen, becoming more and more important, seemed to him to constitute a direct menace to social equilibrium, and at a deeper level, to the safeguarding of spiritual values. Erasmus is alleged to have held asceticism in contempt ; but all the same, we see in him an extreme distrust of money and material things and an ardent desire to lessen as far as possible their influence in the life of society.

The *Institutio principis Christiani*, published in 1516, is naturally the best summary of Erasmus' ideas on this subject. They are similar to those which Thomas More had, the previous year, partly disclosed and partly hidden in his deliberately paradoxical *Utopia*. The kind of government he most approved would be a balanced combination of monarchy, aristocracy, and democracy. The education he proposed for a prince has for its whole aim to uproot in him the fiercely egotistical tendencies whose logical outcome Machiavelli, three or four years earlier, had deduced with complete moral indifference. Erasmus' Prince must be brought up in the conviction that he is nothing other than an instrument of the public weal. Consequently, he must promote, not impair, the well-being of his subjects, bring about the unity of rival classes, and pursue good relations with neighbouring states. He is urged to feed his mind not so much on ancient history which would risk developing a taste for a wholly exterior and superficial greatness, but on the history and particularly the geography of his own country, studied on the spot. The prince should consider himself the first servant of the law, and not use it for his own purposes ; and the law itself should envisage, not an abstract or chimerical goal, but the realization of the best that is, in fact, possible.

Erasmus had no thought of a simple common sharing of the goods of society. He recommended rather a strict discipline in the production and distribution of riches. He believed in a social hierarchy. He did not however believe it should be founded on riches, commerce, industry, or position—he even went so far as to propose means for preventing the concentration of riches in a few owners. He thought that the economy should not only be directed but hedged in by sumptuary laws, safeguarding the simplicity of life which, on spiritual grounds, he held necessary for the common good of humanity. But what seemed to him essential was that there should be an economy founded on peace and not on war ; and, in consequence, tending of its very nature to encourage the one and restrain the other.

We will not follow M. Renaudet in his description of the passionate efforts which Erasmus made, while at Basel, to put these strong convictions of his into practice. He made the greatest possible use of the international prestige his work as a humanist had gained for him. Through his letters and *Apologias*, through the continual additions to his *Colloquies* and *Adages*, and finally in his *Paraphrases* on the Gospels, he never lost an opportunity to place before kings, and even popes, the principles, both Christian and at the same time human, whose theoretical consequences he had striven to elucidate. It was up to them, he said quite frankly, to give these ideas practical application.

More especially did he exert himself to encourage and help in a reconciliation between France and the Empire. In like manner his courteous but decisive refusal to reissue the *De Monarchia* of Dante was due to his fear of the effect it might have in the quarrel between the Emperor and the Pope. When the Ottoman advance became menacing—Vienna itself was in danger in 1526—Erasmus insisted on the necessity, prefatory to any crusade, of a reconciliation and of a rechristianization of Christendom. He did not hestitate to state that without this a crusade would only be another pretext for further expeditions of a most unedifying character ; or else simply a means for establishing an imperial supermonarch, in his eyes utterly valueless.

The Peasants' War, an unforeseen though foreseeable reaction to the Lutheran Reformation in Germany, occasioned some of his most penetrating utterances. He was correct in seeing in this revolt and in its savage repression both a sign and a fresh cause of the prevalent materialistic attitude of mind, showing itself in the increased conviction that right and power belong to brute force alone.[6]

6) pp. 65-121.

CHAPTER X

ERASMUS IN A DIVIDED CHRISTENDOM

WE COME NOW to the chapter which treats specifically of Erasmian theology ; M. Renaudet entitles it *le modernisme érasmien*.[1] He begins by attributing to Erasmus independence of the theological schools in general. Admittedly, he indicates in passing Erasmus' statements on the necessity of not proclaiming the breakdown of scholasticism before finding something to replace it, and his repeated assertions of respect for St. Thomas Aquinas. But M. Renaudet feels that the revelance of the latter should be minimized. He has little difficulty in demonstrating the extent to which both Scotistic dialectic and the logic of the Parisian nominalists could excite the disgust and the acrimony of Erasmus.

Ockham was, again in M. Renaudet's estimation, the only medieval theologian capable to a certain extent of finding favour with Erasmus because of his critical and positivistic tendencies. But what M. Renaudet most insists on is Erasmus's indifference both to the revival of Platonism begun by Petrarch and continued by Ficino, Pico della Mirandola, Rodolphus Agricola and Colet, and to medieval aristotelianism. He shared neither the scientific interest of Aristotle, nor the taste for metaphysical speculation of the platonists. Distrusting, as he did, both naturalism and rationalism, which he saw arising in the neo-aristotelianism

1) pp. 122-188.

of Padua, the illuminism of Ficino and his school
left him cold.

In this independence of his M. Renaudet is inclined to see a combined result of the *devotio moderna*
of Windesheim and classical pyrrhonism. The
infancy and the youth of Erasmus had been dominated
by the former. The latter was the result of his
study of antiquity, and no doubt corresponded with
his natural temperament. Certainly he expected,
sometimes with abounding confidence, to derive
firm and lasting truth from the teachings of antiquity, but not from any system, particularly not
from its metaphysics. Rather did he look for knowledge of the human heart, moral reflections, and
noble examples of virtue wherein lie the imperishable
values of the *Phaedo*, the *Tusculan Orations*, and
Plutarch. Renouncing all metaphysical ambition,
he held that it was by the cultivation of the human
soul that the study of antiquity should lead that of
Christian thought, and then help to bring it to
fruition.

But how and where was one to obtain the teachings
of Christianity ? Erasmus urges us to turn back
to Christian sources, and primarily to the Scriptures,
emancipated, thanks to the methods of humanism,
from lifeless and misleading commentaries.

M. Renaudet follows page by page the major
theses of the *Ratio verae theologiae*. With the Fathers,
Erasmus insists that all the Old Testament leads to
Christ but, in his view, for the most part only
through allegorical interpretation, apart from which
numbers of texts seem void of any profitable teaching.
He insists at the same time, on the authority of
St. Augustine, that not all of Scripture is of equal
value. Even within the New Testament, it seemed
to him, there appeared to be an order of importance,

the first place falling to the Gospels and St. Paul.
In the Old Testament, he gave preference to certain
passages in the prophets, Isaias in particular, and
to the Psalms. But it is obviously the New Testament
that was his chief interest ; besides, it is only there
that his learning was fully competent.

In due course he set about the task of working
out an exegetical method. He insisted for the most
part on the necessity of having recourse to the Greek
(or Hebrew) text. One could not, he said, be content
with the Vulgate. Further, a thorough philological
knowledge of these languages was necessary to
avoid flagrant misinterpretations, such as arose from
simple ignorance of grammar or of precise shades
of meaning. Then he set out a series of criteria, the
first of which is that a citation should never be
detached from its context, nor from the general
thought of its author, nor even from Scripture in
its entirety. Following this came questions regarding
the time, the occasion, the intention, and the tone
of the discourse.

Erasmus devotes a whole disertation, closely
argued and original, to the legitimacy in principle
of an allegorical interpretation authorized by the
example of Christ and of the Apostles. At the same
time, he insists on the extreme prudence which
such usage demands, and the directive principles
without which it is easy to wander off into fantasy,
if not heresy.

Next Erasmus passes over to the exegetes. He
applied himself to estimating and grading the
authority of the different Fathers, putting in the
first rank the Greeks, primarily Origen, and among
the Latins clearly prefering St. Jerome for his concern
for objectivity, rather than St. Augustine and his
exegesis which, in his view, seemed preoccupied with

edifying at all costs.   He does not completely set
aside the scholastics, though he is bitterly censorious
of the idle questions, scarcely related to the text,
in which they had practically buried it.   Questions
of the sort, often insoluble, certainly completely
foreign to the manner of the sacred writing, merely
emptied the Scriptures of the living reality.

In the end, while the preface to his edition of the
New Testament which had appeared in Basel in
1516 enthusiastically recommended the spread of
the Scriptures among the people, his experience
during the following years made him less confident.
Erasmus came to insist more and more upon personal preparation as indispensable for an understanding of the biblical writings, and on the danger
of individual interpretations insufficiently grounded.

Discussing the spirit of Erasmian theology, M.
Renaudet has little difficulty in showing that there
was nothing metaphysical about it, and much less
anything of an apologetic nature.   Erasmus was too
confident that the very sublimity of biblical doctrine
would bring conviction of its truth once the Scriptures were made clear and living.   And this doctrine
for him was centred closely round the person,
teaching, and work of Jesus Christ.   Therein consists
the fundamental object of faith working through
charity, which gradually permeates the whole of
life in imitation of Christ.   In a word, it is the *devotio
moderna* of the Brothers of the Common Life and
of the Canons Regulars of Windesheim.   But it is
likewise this devotion rejuvenated and refashioned
by a study of the Gospels in a new spirit of objectivity.   There is, besides, a marked insistence on a
spirituality profoundly hostile to all religious formalism, to all " judaising " of Christianity.   Erasmus
finally distinguished himself radically from the

Protestants, whom he would almost seem to have agreed with on this point, by proposing as the ideal not indeed faith as opposed to works, but faith translated into life by practical charity.

M. Renaudet sums up the Christianity Erasmus proposes as " a humanist ethic, revised and corrected according to the Gospel." [2] He believes it can be characterized by a favorite phrase of Erasmus : " The philosophy of Christ." " An unusual phrase," says M. Renaudet, " the choice of which is one of the clearest revelations of Erasmian modernism." [3]

On these ideas of his, Erasmus built an interesting conception of Christian history and of the development of dogma and of Christian institutions. He distinguished a first period which was that of the Jewish law ; then an era of prophecy ending with St. John the Baptist ; a third, that of the primitive Church which was noteworthy for the extreme simplicity of its theological formulae, as well as for the incomparable purity and intensity of its life. The fourth period, which began with the conversion of Constantine, was one of triumph and of many-sided developments, but certainly of alteration as well. We are now in the fifth period, predicted by St. Paul ; the Christian spirit degenerates and charity grows cold.

By way of remedy, Erasmus attempted to establish an ideal economy of human society. Priests were to be strangers to the spirit of the world, drawing from its source the pure light of the Gospel, in order to communicate it to the second circle of Christianity, the temporal government, which would in its turn apply this teaching to the third and last

2) P. 147.
3) P. 146.

circle, the Christian people. [4] The function of modern
theology should be to criticize all that sullies the
purity of traditional doctrine by a mixture of non-
assimilated human elements, thereby upsetting the
balance of Christian teaching, or even stifling it
by their ignoble character.

But what was Erasmus's practical conception,
and how did he attempt its realization ? First, he
obtained a critical edition of the biblical text, established in accordance with the manuscripts, by
means of scientific methods then in process of
elaboration. Then, there was to be a new translation
of the scriptures, as exact as possible. Finally, the
notes were to be essentially philological, aiming
solely at an exact understanding of the text itself.
The only commentary, properly speaking, which
he allowed was an elucidation of Scripture by itself—
that is, the comparison of texts with one other and
their mutual clarification.

The disastrous results which seemed to him to
have been brought about by recent developments
within Christianity are detailed in the course of his
writings. They may be arranged under two headings.
Under one comes the substitution of a metaphysic
and more particularly an abstruse dialectic for the
" philosophy of Christ," itself a simple and luminous
doctrine of life. Under the other, the re-intro-
duction under various forms of a completely materialistic religion, bound up with legalism and external
practices, and the disappearance of " true religion,"

4) M. Renaudet has no doubts concerning the patristic sources of these
speculations. On the different eras of history in the prospective of a Christian
see H. de Lubac, S. J. *Catholicism*. We would draw particular attention to a
citation from St. Cyril of Alexandria's *De cultu et adoratione* (P.G. 68, col.
1061 ff).

As for the various stages within Christianity and their interactions, the
source is apparently Pseudo-Denys, *The Ecclesiastical Hierarchy* (P.G. 111,
col. 501). But the great liberties Erasmus took must be kept in mind.

which is the life of the believing and loving soul.

But Erasmus was equally emphatic against the remedies currently proposed for the two evils he denounced. Both the cabalistic, Pythagorean philosophy of Pico della Mirandola, and the neo-Platonism of Ficino, seemed to him as faulty as degenerate scholasticism. What he desired was a return to the Gospel, itself understood in the light of St. Paul. That would ensure salvation as regards practical life ; it would not come from an appeal to a council or revolutionary measures of reform. At all costs, Erasmus desired to avoid these latter measures. The only result they would have was a further deterioration.

Ultimately, prayer was the only recourse so that Christ himself from within, gently, without violence, simply by means of plain preaching and return to the sources, might restore true Christian liberty to fettered minds and captive souls. M. Renaudet rightly emphasises how all of this was opposed to the activities of the Protestant reformers. The difference lies not only in prudence, and in a horror for sudden and brusque change, but even more in his definite assertion of the necessity for the development which had been going on from the very beginning, and of its overall value.

For all that, M. Renaudet feels justified in concluding, *the spirit behind this criticism, so prudent, so respectful of all that is so rarely held, is not Catholic. Erasmus is too loud in his proclamation of the liberty of the Christian, freed from the traditional laws regulating his belief and devotion. He insists too strongly that, in the religious life, only the spirit counts, and that all the rest is indifferent. Quite clearly he only submitted to Roman order for the form's sake, and looked forward to a future where variations of Christian thought would be freely permitted. His indifference to dogmas, whose historical variations he traces, and expects others in the future as necessary, is hard to reconcile with the orthodoxy he always professed. Certainly, he never had either the spirit or the temperament of an heresiarch, but he deplored heresy rather as a moralist, condemning intellectual obstinacy and pride, than as a theologian fighting in the defence of a Church. He sees in philosophical speculation applied outside its own field to the Christian faith the origin of false doctrines, and it is his pyrrhonism rather than his Catholicism which rejects them.*[5] Such is the view of M. Renaudet ; we will examine it later.

*　　　*　　　*

In two long chapters entitled *Erasmus and the Catholic Church*, M. Renaudet returns to the chronological order he departed from to give a general view of Erasmus' works. In so doing, he aims at tracing, in the facts surveyed, the origin or application of the principles we have just assembled.

His first chapter extends from Erasmus' settlement at Basel in the autumn of 1521, to the publication of the *De libero arbitrio* in September 1524. [6] This period is marked by the effort of the Catholics to draw Erasmus into active hostility to the Lutherans by writing against them. We will go into the numerous controversies Erasmus had to conduct against various Catholic opponents from the very beginning of his residence at Basel.

The brief Erasmus received from Pope Adrian VI at the end of January, 1523 assured him of the unalterable confidence of the Holy See and invited

5)　pp. 170-171.
6)　pp. 189-236.

I

him to Rome. But a letter from the papal datary,
accompanying that of the Pope, assumed as only
natural that Erasmus was preparing a great work
against Luther : and the humanist found himself
in a quandary. He began with a confidential letter,
as the pope himself had invited him, and declined
the invitation, on the ground of health. Further, he
emphasised the role he was able to play at Basel,
in close contact with the Lutherans, and making
the best possible use of contacts.

After this opening, he went on to propose the
remedies that seemed to him most efficacious.
Unhappily, this part of his letter has only come
down to us in mutilated form. It insists on the
necessity of not having recourse to violence, which
would only make matters far worse. Instead, Erasmus
suggests offering a large-scale amnesty, and commen-
cing this with a policy of firm opposition to all
revolutionary innovations.

Finally he points out the conditions that would
lead to a reform of the Church itself, which he feels
is the only decisive remedy for the anarchical reformation. One of these conditions is a true detachment on the part of the Church from all secular
authorities as regards material advantages ; the
other, a sincere effort to liberate consciences from
formalism, or from a too heavy legalism, while
taking care not to weaken authority, or dissipate
devotion. For this purpose, Erasmus favoured
the creation of a reforming commission, small in
number, but composed of men possessing an incontestable personal authority, rather than of a
council.

Meanwhile, to gain time, Erasmus decided to
formulate in writing his ideas of the Lutheran
reformation. All the same, the *libellus* he had in

mind at first was not to be a purely cont
treatise against the Lutherans, but to have a
character. He wanted, while definitely but
condemning the wild outbreaks of the Prote ..nts,
to safeguard, against the risk of a pure and simple
reaction, certain of their earlier demands in themselves legitimate. This was his real reason for hesitating so long between the opposing two camps.

Though disagreeing more and more with what
the Lutherans were doing he persisted in believing
that to condemn them and do nothing positive
was to condemn at the same time the hopes of
a true reform which they had stirred up. He there-
fore planned his work as a dialogue between three
persons : one was to speak for Luther ; another
for the intransigent Catholics, while the third would
attempt to mediate between them.

But the announcement of this project failed to
mitigate the furious onslaughts directed from Spain,
France and the Low Countries, and merely served
to alienate the Lutherans so much that he no longer
felt safe in Basel. Realizing that events had out-
stripped him, he abandoned his projected work.
Resolved to hesitate no longer, perhaps owing to
the pressing counsel of Thomas More from whom
he had only just received a letter, now lost, Erasmus
confided to the Dominican John Schmidt, in November 1523, his final decision. He would attack Luther
on the subject of free will. After a very long silence
on the part of Pope Adrian VI to whom he had
written his intentions, a silence which caused him
some uneasiness, Erasmus had finally received most
comforting reassurances. The Pope urged him
strongly to develop the ideas he had outlined. Unhappily, at the very moment when he was receiving
this news, the Pope died.

Clement VII, however, was no sooner on the throne than he reiterated his confidence. But Erasmus still hesitated before making public his new intention. Finally, on February 13, 1524, he announced his projected book to the Pope. The response arrived on April 3, in a letter composed by Sadoleto which announced that the Pope had imposed silence on certain of Erasmus' most violent Catholic opponents. In the beginning of September, Froben put on sale the first copies of *On Free Will*, written and printed in record time.

On this work of capital importance so often commented upon, M. Renaudet does not try to say anything very new. He shows merely how the choice of subject fitted in so well with Erasmus' own preoccupations as outlined in the preceding chapter. He thus briefly summarises its teaching : " Erasmus dismisses at once the excessive confidence of Pelagius in man's moral strength and the final condemnation passed on man by the Augustinians and by Luther. He outlines an intermediate solution which assigns to grace the rôle of moving the soul and showing it the way, and the glory of crowning its effort, and grants the soul at least the merit of its effort and daily progress." [7]

The extreme moderation of the *De libero arbitrio* did not appease the enemies whom Erasmus had in Catholic theological circles, and only produced a violent explosion on the part of Luther himself in his *De servo arbitrio*, which was published in December, 1525.

From the end of 1524 to the date of his departure from Basel, Erasmus was chiefly occupied in a long conflict with the theological faculty of Paris. To it M. Renaudet's sixth chapter is mainly devoted.

7)   p. 234.

Fairly moderate in tone at the outset against Noel Beda, the syndic of the Sorbonne, it developed into the most stubborn warfare Erasmus ever had to wage. It was marked by three successive censures pronounced against him by the Sorbonne— the first that Erasmus had ever received from an ecclesiastical body. In May, 1526, in the course of the first legal process brought against Berquin, his translator, the *Colloquies* of Erasmus were condemned. On December 17, 1527, a still graver censure was passed against several passages in his *Paraphrases*. On July 17, 1528, the preceding censures were repeated in stronger forms.

What should be noted however is that this unfortunate affair all turned on misconceptions. The texts judged by the Sorbonne were translations made by Berquin. Only when it was too late Erasmus discovered that they distorted and misrepresented his thought in a definitely Lutheran sense. [8]

Then, in the summer of 1527, in the midst of this controversy, Erasmus found himself attacked no less violently by some Spanish monks at the Conference of Valladolid. But this ended in at least a momentary triumph for the Erasmians. Then from Rome, with Erasmus hardly recovered from the terrible difficulties of the previous year, Clement VII sent another letter (dated July 16). While still favourable to Erasmus, it yet, for the first time, ordered his books to be examined.

During these years Erasmus seemed discouraged and utterly weary. The excesses of the reformers seemed to him to have given fresh life to the evils within the Church which, at first, he thought Luther might have aided in abolishing. Luther, said Erasmus, addressed himself to the defence of Christian liberty,

8)   cf. p. 305.

but the only and inevitable result of his work has been to restrict its domain more than ever. " This tyranny of princes, of prelates and of monks, as you love to call it, you have not suppressed but intensified," he wrote in the first of his *Hyper-aspistes* :

> Everything that anyone now says, all that a man does, now serves as a pretext for suspicions. On all we had hitherto been free to discuss, we hardly dare open our mouths. The slavery you had thought of suppressing has been redoubled. [9]

At the same time, although he does not seem to have had doubts about his own personal principles, he reproached himself more and more for having lacked prudence in their application, fearing that he may have given involuntary support to a mis-judged reform more and more antipathetic to him. A letter of his says :

> At one time I wrote in the cause of spiritual liberty (referring to his *Enchirideon militis Christiani*). I did so in all sincerity, for I never expected anything like this new genera-tion. I had hoped that the role of ceremonies would have been diminished in favour of true piety. But they have been so brutally rejected that in place of liberty of spirit there has come about a liberty of the flesh without restraint. [10]

M. Renaudet's last chapter shows mainly the successive stages in the deliberate separation Erasmus made between his cause and that of the reformers of Wittemberg, during his years in Basel.

In a letter written to Duke George of Saxony on

9) p. 261.

10) p. 302.

September 3, 1522, Erasmus vigorously maintains that the first Lutheran protests are well founded ; but he also indicates his other view, since from the form assumed by the movement almost from the beginning and from the attitude of the reformer himself, he could look for no more than the ruin of the hopes he had originally entertained. Then there was the incident of Hutten's pamphlet, published in Strasbourg in April or May of 1523. In his response in the Spongia, Erasmus, still without radically condemning Luther, formulates a series of criticisms wherein he clearly distinguishes the reform which had been called for in his avowals from what had been put into effect at Wittemberg.

Then, in April 1524, Luther tried, with remarkable clumsiness, to gain at least the neutrality of this possible adversary, by a combination of cringing and rudeness. Erasmus' dignified answer left him but little hope. In his turn, Erasmus, at the time of the appearance of the *De libero arbitrio*, made overtures to Melanchthon. He explained the conciliatory purpose of his book, while criticising the insolent dogmatism and the increased disorder which were the only visible effects of the pretended reform until then. Despite Melanchthon's own moderation, nothing came of this.

In the beginning of 1525, his advice to the magistrates of Basel on the practical questions of reform emphasised the quarrel. In the eyes of Erasmus, there could not be any question of true reform without the express approbation of ecclesiastical authority.[11] That same year, and again at the request of the counsellors of Basel, he opposed courteously but categorically the new opinion of Œcolampadius on the Eucharist. In December, at Wittemberg, appeared

11) p. 330.

Luther's *De servo arbitrio* with an effect like a delayed-action bomb. Overwhelmed with insults, Erasmus, in a final letter to the reformer dated April 11, 1526, testified in moderate but unanswerable terms to his own good conscience and his certainty that Luther by his own fault had ruined the work he might have achieved.[12] In February, 1526, the first of Erasmus' *Hyperaspistes*, while defending the position taken by Erasmus, refused to admit a divorce between Scripture and tradition, or between an invisible Church which is alone holy, and the visible one.

Already, with his habitual perspicuity, Erasmus foresaw the imminent downfall of the new dogmatism. That same year, his *Prestigiarum detectio* reaffirms the constancy of his faith in the traditional doctrine of the Eucharist. Then in August, 1527, the second book of the *Hyperaspistes*, more maturely thought out than the first part, opposed the paradoxical theology of Luther's *De servo arbitrio* where it clearly issues in a double predestination, with a Christian humanism that is and remains the true Erasmian theology. The last bridges are now cut. As the Reformation had meanwhile been definitely established at Basel, the departure of Erasmus was only a matter of time. On April 13, 1529, as we have seen, he left the city.[13]

12) p. 338.
13) pp. 305-360.

CHAPTER XI

WAS ERASMUS A " MODERNIST " BEFORE THE EVENT ?

WITH THIS EVENT, M. Renaudet brings his work to a close, faithful to his intention of avoiding a definite conclusion and of confining his studies to a strictly limited sphere. This does not however, as we have seen, prevent the emergence, all through the book, of frequent suggestions as to the position of Erasmus both as regards the Church and the Reformation. In consequence, the conclusions he never expressly formulates stand out with the utmost clarity, particularly in the chapter entitled " Erasmian Modernism."

Furthermore, even if M. Renaudet, by the very nature of his inquiry, had determined not to come to more precise conclusions, it may still be asked whether he had not already fixed on them in advance in his introduction.[1] Erasmus is made to be the discreet initiator of a rationalist spirituality, empty of dogma, of a laicised Christian morality, illuminated only by the kind of vague mystic fervour beloved of the Enlightenment. In spite of this, his clear-sighted prudence, and particularly his profound sense of history and its continuity, managed to hold back this basically radical evolutionism from hastening the break with traditional Christianity. The moderation of the humanist, however, included, as one of its elements, the unavowed conviction that the rupture would come about of

1) cf. pp. xvii-xviii : " The author of the *Enchiridion*, etc . . ." to " restraining the liberty of the children of God."

itself, and all the better if allowed to happen without disturbance.

It should be remarked at once that this presentation of Erasmian theology is by no means new. It only makes more precise what is commonly accepted, at least since the eighteenth century. It is to be found indiscriminately among both anti-Catholic controversialists and too hasty apologists.

The finest compliment that one can pay the work of M. Renaudet is to say that it seems all along to be leading to a number of fresh insights. But, we are bound to add, after the Introduction just mentioned, the book, however conscientious, seems to have been written to support a definite thesis. To speak more precisely, certain *a priori* judgements seem to have given an unfortunate twist to the development of a criticism otherwise scrupulous and fair. We can see emerging unconsciously a *petitio principii* from his use of an unfortunate word. Whether we like it or not, the term " modernism " which M. Renaudet employs has in the recent history of ideas acquired a special significance which makes it dangerous to use as he does. He adopts this expression to designate the effort by which Erasmus attempted to assimilate the intellectual acquisitions of the age into his Christianity.

But from that use of the term we pass imperceptibly to the kind of nebulous philosophy redolent of the atmosphere at the end of the nineteenth century. Finally, there is imputed to this same religious philosophy a vagueness in everything but its negations, simply, it would appear, because he had proposed in his time to take on a task similar to that which the " modernists " had wanted to accomplish, some two generations ago. But we fail to see that this conclusion has any serious foundation, other than the equivocal use of a term which bears two meanings. On careful reading, it seems to us that this drift accompanies the whole course of M. Renaudet's work, and results from a succession of inexactitudes we must now discuss.

We begin with a very general criticism. In reading certain works of authorities well-versed, as is M. Renaudet in historical criticism, we are often astonished at coming up against a fact which unfortunately seems unquestionable. Whereas such scholars, in dealing with a question of ancient philosophy or religion, take the utmost care not to affirm anything unless it is supported by texts scientifically interpreted, yet as soon as it is a matter of Catholic dogma, they are content to make all sorts of vague assertions without giving any reference at all. One can easily imagine where this leads when it comes to defining the attitude to the Church of a thinker, himself subtle enough in expression.

Quite early in the book, one detail puts us on our guard. M. Renaudet admits as obvious the belief of Erasmus in the Immaculate Conception, merely referring us to another part of his own work. But we find there, in the number of Erasmian texts cited, nothing to substantiate this affirmation. On the other hand, we see there many indications of the belief of Erasmus in the virgin birth of Christ. It is hard to resist the suspicion that M. Renaudet has confused the two dogmas, different as they are, when a glance at any ordinary catechism would have saved him from the mistake. This hardly inspires us with confidence when he comes to the heart of the problem, which is to mark off clearly what is orthodox and what is heterodox in Erasmian theology. On what criteria can M. Renaudet be basing his judgment, if he shows himself so confused

and mistaken on a point of Catholic dogma
such as this ?

In his Introduction, we find him, in fact, brushing
aside a grave objection with a single remark. To
the continual approval shown Erasmus by the Popes,
M. Renaudet opposes a condemnation by the
faculties of theology and by several priests. We
can pass over the fact that on the testimony of
M. Renaudet's book it was the faculty of Paris
alone that at this epoch condemned Erasmus, and
this was done solely upon the perusal of a translation of his work M. Renaudet himself shows to
have been erroneous. Besides this, there are the
condemnations brought against him by individual
theologians. But they speak for no one but themselves. In any case, what sort of Catholicism is this,
on what basis can one pass judgment on the position
of the humanist while wholly discounting the authority of the pope in comparison with that of theological
faculties, admittedly of distinction, or even as compared with a crowd of mere controversialists ?

We notice, too, early in the book, a strange
mention of " canonical " epistles of St. Paul, opposed
to his " authentic " (*sic*) Epistles, and to the Epistle
to the Hebrews.[2]   These details, to which many
more could easily be added, give a very dubious
impression of the critical procedure used by M.
Renaudet.

All through the work, the suspicion is forced upon
the reader that the author only admits as truly
Catholic the opinions of the most reactionary.
When, too, he comes across a clear sign of welcome
to modern ideas, even in a pope, and expressed
in the most solemn of documents, M. Renaudet

2)   This is to say nothing of his " High Church " on p. 71 which really
refers to the higher clergy.

sees in it nothing more than individual temerity, contrary to the spirit of the Church. In view of principles so gratuitous and so vacillating, we cannot help wondering if it was worth using so much industry to arrive at conclusions already formed.

What is still worse is that M. Renaudet, after citing an authoritative text to define the Church's attitude, goes on to manipulate the text, to twist it to yield the interpretation he needs. There is only one papal text contemporaneous with Erasmus and that expresses serious reserve on his opinions : " Libros ipsos Erasmi . . . examines ; si vero aliquos evangelicam doctrinam atque fidem orthodoxam non sapere aut ab illo errore repereris, illos non legendos esse declares." This injunction couched in very hypothetical terms suggesting the unlikelihood of error in Erasmus becomes a categorical assertion of error in the paraphrase of M. Renaudet : " certain books of Erasmus can be read without danger ; others are prohibited." [3]

But in comparison with this distortion of the whole setting, the attempts made to retouch or adjust the words of Erasmus correspondingly are still more amazing. While M. Renaudet unduly simplifies the Catholicism in whose context he places Erasmus, making it altogether too fixed and rigid, he twists page after page of his writings into the opposite of their real meaning, and so manages to detect a revolutionary sense in the most innocent common-places. The task of tracing out these distortions is delicate, and may be tiresome, but is justified by the importance of the result.

We had best begin by returning to the statement

3) In the letter of Clement VII to the Inquisitor Manrique dated July 16, 1527 (Allen, VII, 1846, pp. 17-21).

which we have already noted without comment :
" Erasmus," says M. Renaudet, " gives his theology
the decidedly classical designation of philosophy
of Christ. It is not a usual name, and his choice of
it is one of the more obvious signs of Erasmian
modernism."[4]   M. Renaudet goes on to insist
on the scandal this expression would have given
not merely to the spiritual brethren of Windersheim,
or to the great scholastics, but even to Marsiglio
Ficino.[5] But this obvious sign of Erasmian modernism is nothing more than a deliberate archaism.
Erasmus borrowed it from the ordinary usage of
the Greek Fathers, particularly of those he liked
best, the Alexandrians and the Cappadocians. With
them it had a deliberately paradoxical sense, and
was directed against the profane philosophies. It
is the equivalent of the wisdom of Christ, of which
St. Paul speaks, when he says that it is foolishness
to the Greeks and a scandal to the Jews. If anything is obvious, it is that Erasmus is using this
expression in the same way, opposing the doctrine
of life in the Gospel to the trivialities of a decadent
scholasticism.

The same thing can be said for his use of the word
sermo as an equivalent of *logos*.   M. Renaudet
understands this as a rejection of tradition.[6]   But
again, it is, on the contrary, an archaism. Erasmus
is turning back to the language of the first Latin
Fathers, and in particular to Tertullian. One of
the main supports of the alleged Erasmian modernism
turns out to be merely a crude misunderstanding.

4)   p. 146.

5)   To insist on the naivety by which in contrast he sees Christianity in
the title of Ficino's *Theologia platonica* would be cruel. But in fact, the
De mundo and even the treatises of Plutarch were precisely " theologies "
for the ancients.

6)   p. 25, cf. p. 158.

This is the case, too, in another matter of no little importance. Frequently, M. Renaudet speaks as if Erasmus was proposing to prune the dogmas of the Church. But any reader aware of the precise meaning of the word dogma in traditional Catholic terminology will immediately recognize in almost every paragraph of this account a confusion that is hardly credible. M. Renaudet, in fact, includes under that term both dogmas properly so called—that is, solemn definitions of the Church—and the ordinary opinions of theological schools. He seems, too, to concern himself chiefly with questions of fifteenth century scholasticism that Erasmus cites and discards as idle ones. In one place, for example, M. Renaudet speaks of the " dogmatism of theologians," then of the law of Christ made hard and burdensome "through the doings of men, of their institutions, and their dogma," all expressions belonging to his own vocabulary, we might remark, and not to that of Erasmus.

Then, under the crude title, " Deformity of Belief," our commentator summarises in a few rough sentences one of the most carefully worded passages of Erasmus. In the passage in question, Erasmus points to the following sequence : the primitive form of the faith as given by Christ, the elementary creed of the Apostles, the more complex but necessary definitions made by the Church in view of heresies, and finally the refinements and subleties of rival scholastics which tended to monopolize the stage. But whereas Erasmus took the utmost care to distinguish these in order to oppose the definitions of the Church, which he accepted, to the arbitrary pronouncements of certain theologians which he rejected, M. Renaudet seems equally intent on frustrating his purpose. He finally quotes

examples of how Erasmus writes apropos of the
pope : " Is his power equal to or above that of St.
Peter ? Can he give orders to the angels ? Could
he empty Purgatory at a word ? Is he simply a
man, or almost a God ; or does he, like Christ,
participate in two natures ? " [7] A few pages further
on, in drawing his conclusions, M. Renaudet gives
us his first article of the Erasmian programme :
" To set minds free from rigid and lifeless dogmas,
abstract and sterile systems built up by the dialectical ingenuity of theologians." Again he returns
to the point : " The Erasmian reform," he writes,
" guided by Erasmian modernism, destroyed the
Jewish system of imposed dogmas and obligatory
observances . . . . " But there is nothing to substantiate such striking affirmations beyond the
quotations cited above—that is to say, absolutely
nothing. The confusion which reigns here, between
dogma and what is erroneously equated with it,
destroys the very basis of the argument.

This part of the book contains another confusion
closely connected with the first. M. Renaudet
rightly emphasised the importance attributed by
Erasmus to the idea of the development of dogma.
This idea gradually forced itself upon him in the
course of his polemic with the Lutherans. But then
comes the conclusion which M. Renaudet makes
bold to draw : " Dogma, essentially incapable
of expressing the truth of a fact that surpasses
human intelligence, has for Erasmus no more than
historical and provisional value." [8] And he adds
the totally gratuitous conclusion which we have
already quoted : " His indifference to dogmas,
whose history he traces, and whose further variations

7) cited on p. 167.
8) p. 169.

he expects as necessary, is hard to reconcile with the orthodoxy he always professed." It is astonishing to find that M. Renaudet does not furnish one single quotation to justify such assertions. After going carefully through the texts, we can say with perfect safety that there is not a single passage in Erasmus that supports this interpretation. The truth lies in just the opposite direction. Erasmus introduced the idea of development to affirm against the reformers that the truths of faith cannot be limited to the scriptural formulae. As a general principle, in his view, it is impossible to restrict what the divine spirit wishes to make known or to have practised by the Church to what is found explicitly in the New Testament. *Fieri potest ut non omnia semel aperuerit Christi Spiritus Ecclesiae.* This perfectly clear text is cited by M. Renaudet himself.[9] How then can he write after this that Erasmus calls dogmas in which even Luther believed " obscure and uncertain " simply because Erasmus shows that they cannot be established without recourse to tradition?[10]

This inversion of the main principle of Erasmus's thought has a corresponding effect in its applications. Thus M. Renaudet manages to detect a rationalistic doubt on the dogma of transubstantiation in the very terms in which Erasmus undoubtedly seeks to justify the definition : " Transubstantiationem sero definivit Ecclesia ; diu satis erat credere sive sub pane consecrato, sive quocumque modo adesse verum corpus Christi. Ubi rem propius contemplata est, ubi exactius expendit, certius praescripsit."[11]

9) on p. 169, n. 3 (cf. Allen IV, 1006, 192-193).

10) pp. 339-340.

11) pp. 171-172.

J

Along with these flagrant errors, we come upon inferences and even additions still more difficult to account for. In the *Hyperaspistes* which was Erasmus' reply to the Lutherans, "Fero igitur hanc Ecclesiam, donec videro meliorem," is obviously, from the context, a joking way of saying,—"Until you can show me a better, (with the implication that such was unlikely) the Catholic Church will suffice for me." But in the exegesis of M. Renaudet, this becomes : "an admission of one whose eyes had been opened and who at last saw through the deceit."[12] M. Renaudet turns into a threat of defection a single expression which Erasmus used to defend himself from the charge of dabbling with heresy, and which simply meant that he could have added to the power it already had, had he chosen to support it.

A passage where Erasmus, speaking of Œcolampadius's acute reasoning against the dogma of the Eucharist, says : "ita ut seduci posse videantur etiam electi . . ." means, according to M. Renaudet that "he acknowledges the conclusions of Œcolampadius to be almost convincing." Nor is M. Renaudet very happy with the biblical allusions in which Erasmus abounds. They escape him every time ; and with them, goes the meaning of the whole sentence. Erasmus asks why uneducated monks bore themselves in chanting the Psalms without understanding them at all. He answers ironically : "Quia spiritu canunt, non mente" alluding to I *Cor*. 15 : 15. But his commentator gravely explains for us, not having caught the allusion : "Erasmus' interpretation is much more intellectualist than that of Lefévre, who admits

12) p. 260.

no opposition between ' spiritus ' and ' mens.' "[13] This is simply ridiculous.

But what is more serious is that apropos of a controversy between the prince of Carpi, brother-in-law of Pico della Mirandola, and Erasmus, M. Renaudet begins by characterising the position which Erasmus rejected as " an obstinate conservatism admitting no doubt about any point of dogma." In fact, there is here no question of dogma, but of simple liturgical practice or discipline, as the context clearly demonstrates. But this is nothing to what follows. Giving a list of the practices which Erasmus cites as primitive, though with no desire for their return, M. Renaudet inserts this : " The reduction of the Eucharist to a simple commemoration." Now the text actually reads : " Eucharistiam domi summendam " which means of course " to take communion at home".[14]

Here is an analogous example. Erasmus speaks of the new laws—" leges novae "—which were introduced into the Christian community after the close of the persecutions " quarum aliquot viderentur cum Christi decretis pugnare . . . " But M. Renaudet makes him say outright " new rules which appear at times to introduce into the corpus of Christian doctrine an obvious contradiction with the precepts of Christ."[15] Finally, Erasmus recalls—speaking hypothetically, and reminding Luther of his own words—" the tyranny of princes, of prelates and of monks," but M. Renaudet has no hesitation in adding to the text " and of theologians."[16]

After this, we are not surprised to find M. Renaudet representing as " singularly rash " criticisms, pieces

13) p. 201, n. 4.
14) Leyden edition, t. IX. 1109A.
15) p. 251.
16) p. 261.

of exegesis far in advance of the age, but which the most scrupulously orthodox theologians of today accept without question. What can be said about such an extraordinary statement as this : " The Master, both divine and familiar, whom he (Erasmus) reverences most profoundly is not without certain resemblances to the Jesus of Renan "? There seems to be no basis for this statement other than the commonsense observation of Erasmus that " the person of Jesus in the Gospels is always enveloped in mystery." [17]

These glaring misjudgments, the result of continual, and, we can only hope, unconscious, transpositions, show strikingly the constant violence M. Renaudet does to the texts. The very terms he uses show that M. Renaudet, despite his extensive learning, has not achieved the objectivity so essential to his work. Erasmus is so evidently one of the fathers of the modern spirit (and perhaps the most illustrious) that a modern writer is perforce tempted to make him the father of his own convictions and to ascribe to him his own strong prejudices.

The *Ratio verae theologiae,* in particular, expresses in decisive fashion what is best and newest in our historical criticism. Anyone who, for his own part, considers the acceptance of this critical spirit as necessarily linked to the rejection of traditional Christianity, is only too strongly inclined to attribute the same connection to Erasmus. What we have said should be enough to show that this connection is absent from the work of Erasmus, and is merely read into it.

Before continuing with the intellectual portrait of Erasmus, we will say, at this point, what, after the necessary corrections, remains of the most

17) p.XXIV ; cf. p. 162.

valuable observations of M. Renaudet. We think the attempt must be given up to make Erasmus the father of modernism, of its evolutionism, and all the more of its symbolo-fideism. On the contrary, our study of him thus far shows him undoubtedly the chief creator of what is today termed positive theology. We mean by this, in the first place, that he brought to light, at a time when a dialectical system was wholly engaged on erecting a structure of questionable deductions on an ever narrowing basis, the incomparable riches of what theologians call the " facts of revelation." Through this his humanism reopened widely the permanent sources of Christian teaching. But the true value of this is seen only in the light of a most important fact, namely, that Erasmus was one of the first to have possessed and applied to the field of theology a true sense of history.[18] In other words he knew how to restore and present the doctrinal riches of Christianity as so many living realities, rather than as mere notions in a fossilised state.

He is likewise very much a modern in his lack of interest in metaphysics and his passionate interest in a psychological ethics. He was naturally averse from speculative theology ; and his contempt for decadent scholasticism alienated him still more. Yet he showed repeatedly a strong liking for the Greek Fathers, particularly for Origen and, surprisingly, for the Pseudo-Areopagite. This suggests that a less reasoned and more contemplative theology would have aroused his interest. In any case his interior life was certainly completely different from the kind of liberal Protestantism generally imputed to him.

18) See P. Sertillanges' contention that the lack of this sense was the great deficiency of the Middle Ages (*Le Christianisme et les philosophies*, vol. 1, pp. 353-354).

Besides, M. Renaudet, and others as well, makes too much of a remark of Colet as a reason for neglecting the connections between the thought of Erasmus and Thomism. His expression of regard cannot be accounted as simple precaution, for at no other time was St. Thomas less valued in the Church. As Père Chenu has shown, thomists and humanists formed at the beginning of the Renaissance a common front against nominalism.[19]　And we might add that the political philosophy of Erasmus, which M. Renaudet has shown owes nothing to either the ancients or to his contemporaries, is quite close to that of St. Thomas. Their respective views of the ideal form of government are identical in so many points that it is difficult to attribute this to pure coincidence.

To sum up, what is most striking in Erasmus is his interest in the human aspect of Christianity, and more precisely in the way it impinges on the life of man, individual or social, particularly when he is seen as a personal thinker, and not only as revealing the letter and spirit of Christian writings. No doubt this is what makes him most representative of his age. But, regret or lament it as one may, the fact remains that this man who symbolises better than anyone the renewal of the world and of ideas characteristic of his epoch performed, at the same time, the function of its Christian conscience. His was the most extensive and coherent attempt his age had seen to present it with a fresh statement of the moral principles and of a Christianity itself, if not always new in conception, at least newly expressed. The merit of his attempt remains, no matter what one may think of its results.

As to these results, it remain for us to study them

19)　*Une Ecole de théologie : le Saulchoir* (Paris: 1937) pp. 27-28.

more closely. Although the judgment passed by M. Renaudet seems to us quite untenable, his book is, at any rate, a most valuable guide through the maze of events with which the thought of Erasmus was concerned. There, in its living context, we will try to examine it afresh and discover its real structure.

BOOK IV

THE THEOLOGY OF ERASMUS

PROFITING BY THE admirable way in which M. Renaudet has recreated the intellectual atmosphere
in which Erasmus worked, we intend to take up
on fresh lines the delicate task of presenting his
thought, and more particularly his theology, its
very soul. For it is here that, in our opinion, M.
Renaudet's work breaks down, ill-served by an
inadequate grasp of the facts of tradition always
present to Erasmus, and misdirected by the wish
to find in him what, indeed, his works may have
occasioned, but which they, in our view, by no means
originated.

Now that the figure of Erasmus as the forerunner,
even the first herald, of an anti-dogmatic liberalism
is seen to be no more than a mirage, we can apply
ourselves wholly to discovering the correct synthesis
of fidelity to tradition and receptiveness to renewal
which characterises his whole position. But our
main concern is not so much to specify each element
found therein as to catch, if possible, in actual life,
the theology of Erasmus, for it was indeed less a
fixed system than a balance of contrasting tendencies.

We shall not try to cover the whole work of
Erasmus here in these few pages. Such an enterprise
is not required by the end in view. Erasmus, in
fact, has himself left a systematic account of the
principles of his theology, or rather, of the ideas
at its source, for there is no question here of any
sort of abstractions. This is his *Ratio, sive Methodus
verae theologiae.* We will go over it again, with less
haste perhaps than did M. Renaudet. But above all
we will take the utmost care to present each problem
in the aspect which Erasmus himself envisaged in
his treatment, rather than run the risk of distorting
his thought by attempting to disengage what we

think is lasting from what seems ephemeral.

To make certain we are not misled by seeing only one aspect of our author, which has resulted in so many divergent interpretations of him, we will compare the contents of this book with those of a completely different one, namely his *Colloquies*. This slender volume, which, however, he was continually expanding, seems indeed to have been the one of all his writings Erasmus cared for most. Its importance does not lie in the theses it upholds, for they are few, and anyone who confined himself to it would have but slight acquaintance with the thought of Erasmus. But nowhere else is the real spirit of Erasmus so truly portrayed. And it is above all else the inner spirit of the man that we are in search of, which will shed light on the more impersonal ideas of the *Ratio verae theologiae*. Nor will we fail to explain these works in the light of the correspondence classified and arranged for the first time by M. Renaudet.

CHAPTER XII

THE *RATIO VERAE THEOLOGIAE*

WHAT EXACTLY IS the scope of the *Ratio*? It is nothing
so ambitious as a treatise on theology in itself
and on what constitutes it. Like many of the works
of Erasmus, it is a manual for students. Today we
would call it an "Introduction to Theological Studies."

The first pages insist strongly that theology is
not only a sacred science because of its object, but
also because of the subjective dispositions which
it requires of its very nature. In the first place it
calls for a *catharsis*, as the ancients would have said,
a moral purification in those approaching it. Theology is no mere matter of technique. Anyone who
does not begin by fostering within himself truly
religious dispositions, and who does not come to
it with a desire for personal betterment, will not
achieve real progress. For theology, as Erasmus
makes bold to say, is a strictly prophetic work.
On this score it demands of its practitioners a special
infusion of the divine spirit. Hence this forceful
exhortation : " Hic primus et unicus tibi sit scopus,
hoc votum, hoc unum age ut muteris, ut rapiaris,
ut affleris ut transformeris in ea quae discis."[1]
So he reaches his first conclusion : " Ita denum
tibi videare profecisse, non si disputes acrius, sed
si te senseris paulatim alterum fieri."[2] He goes on

1) col. 77B : " Your sole and primary aim, your only desire should be so
to work that you may be changed, inspired, even transformed into that which
you are studying." (References to Erasmus' works cited as *col.* refer to the
Le Clerc edition (Leyden : 1703-1706).

2) col. 77C : " In the end you will be able to judge your progress, not by
your ability to argue sharply, but by whether or not you are changed in some
way."

to devote some attention to the deplorable effects of a theology which is merely controversial in tone.

It is easy to see the underlying criticism, which comes out fully later on, of what scholastic theology had become in the course of the fourteenth and fifteenth centuries. But it is important, too, to stress the positive counterpart. Of course, we know him with that trenchant mind of his like that of Lucian ; it stands out clearly even in youthful writings, and was to persist to the very end. But for all that, we must not overlook the profoundly religious spirit seen, at times, even in his polemical works. When this spirit is given full rein, the impression given is all the stronger in that Erasmus' habitual restraint in the words he chooses means that they are to be given their full force.

It has been remarked that this idea of theology makes of Erasmus much more a disciple of the Brothers of Windesheim than he would have willingly acknowledged. But we would emphasise no less how close these views of his are to those found among the Fathers, particularly of the fourth century. We might go even further and say that the first pages of the *Ratio* were directly influenced by the theological sermons of St. Gregory Nazianze. The importance of this is that, if it be true, it follows that his opposition to controversial theology, even though directed at the scholasticism of the sixteenth century, cannot serve as an argument to relegate this noble work of Erasmus to the rank of a mere polemic. This anti-dialectical theme is already present in the Fathers whence Erasmus drew his inspiration. It is of a piece with the religious, we might even say prophetical, conception of theology Erasmus sought to restore. The presence of this element in his work cannot be held to imply that

the developments accompanying it were a mere
pretext for it.

As to the details of the intellectual equipment
the theologian should have, Erasmus begins with
the need for three languages : Latin, Greek and
Hebrew. He pointedly rejects the sophistical argument that Latin was sufficient. On the contrary
he points out : 1) the inaccuracies of existing translations : 2) those which even the best versions could
not avoid : and 3), the impossibility of a truly
critical use of the latter by those who could not
go over the procedure for themselves.

He then passes on to the necessity of what we
would term today general culture for the pursuit
of a true theology. He insists again and again on
the necessity of a knowledge of the natural world,
of rhetoric, and of the poets. This may appear
somewhat unimpressive as being simply a reversion
to the notion of theology as a mere explanation
of Scripture, and to the idea of culture as a mere
preparation for theology, common to those who
wrote before the thirteenth century.

But Erasmus at once gives his reason for this
oldfashioned view. He is once more simply re-
flecting the Fathers. This part of the work, in fact,
leads him to a comparison of the Fathers and the
scholastics, in which the latter hardly appear to
advantage. But the real fault Erasmus finds in them
is that they do not look for the true meaning of the
biblical texts, but instead try to make use of them
in problems that were not the concern of the sacred
authors. The examples he cites show abundantly
that he was not impugning scholasticism indiscriminately and in general, but the Nominalists, as
will be seen later. And even so he concludes with
the words : " Neque vero haec eo dixerim quod

damnem ea studia quae nunc fere videmus in publicis
scholis solennia, modo sobrie casteque tractentur :
neque sola tamen—Nor is this to say that I would
condemn those studies which we see almost constantly in the public schools, provided they be soberly
and sanely conducted ; and that they should not
be the only ones."

This brings him to a third section in which he
gives a summary of his excellent rules of interpretation which we have already commented upon
in the company of M. Renaudet. He does not,
however, propose them before stressing the interest
which a completely objective account of the content
of the Epistles and the Gospels should have as a
guide for the novice theologian. There follow these
questions : " Quid dicatur, verum etiam quo
dicatur, cui dicatur, quibus verbis dicatur, quo
tempore, quo occasione, quid praecedat, quid con-
sequatur."[3] The next part brings out closely the
meaning and bearing of this passage. Then after
a passage excursus on the three divisions of Christian
people and their normal relationships, Erasmus
goes on to express his opinion concerning the use
to be made of the doctors in interpreting the Scriptures. He denies that they can, by any means, be
dispensed with. But he proposes this principle :
" Nulli sic addictos esse oportet, ut nefas esse
ducamus alicubi dissentire—To no one should
we be so attached as to consider it wrong to dissent
from him on some particular point." It is here
that he makes precise the distinction between dogma
and the opinions of the doctors. We would observe
that the reading of this passage is quite enough to

3) cf. The *De decretis Nicaenae Synodus* of Athanasius and the *Contra
Eunomium* of Basil.

refute the more or less radical anti-dogmatism some
have charged him with.

This naturally leads Erasmus to what is the most
important part of his book, both by reason of its
extended treatment and on account of the passionate
intensity he shows. Christ is its object ; and we
see there the idea emerging that while theology is
before all else an explanation of the Scriptures,
it is essentially the knowledge of Christ and His
work.

He starts by laying the foundation for what we
may call an apologetic of Christ. In the first place,
Christ is, as it were, the focus of the whole biblical
teaching : in one way or another the sacred books
all speak of Him. To anyone looking below the
surface, it is evident that fundamentally their subject
is Christ. Their various differences are not minimised,
but rather make their unanimous agreement about
his person so much the more striking.

A further argument is provided by the very life
of Christ and by his teachings. The manner in which
Erasmus elaborates this deserves particular attention:
" Reperies fortassis in Platonis aut Senecae libris
quae non abhorreant a decretis Christi ; reperies
in vita Socratis, quae utcumque cum vita Christi
consentiant ; at circulum hunc, et omnium rerum
inter se congruentium harmoniam in solo Christo
reperies—You will perhaps find in the works of
Plato or of Seneca certain things which are not
opposed to the decrees of Christ; you will find in
the life of Socrates certain things which accord
with the life of Christ. But it is only in Christ that
you will find the full circle and all things gathered
together in harmony." What is noticeable is the
characteristic stamp which Erasmus imprints on this
argument taken from the apologists and Clement

K

of Alexandria. He is not content to say that one
can find assembled in the Gospels truths lying
scattered among the writings of the philosophers.
He brings this abstract argument into life by introducing into it the figure of Christ himself. It is in
this context that a passage of Erasmus which has
been much misused should be read, since it contains
an expression whose omission could easily change
the whole meaning : " Nec fortassis absurdum
fuerit, in sacris quoque voluminibus ordinem auc-
toritatus aliquem constituere : id qod facere non
est veritus Augustinus—Nor would it perhaps be
absurd to set up a certain order of authority in the
sacred books ; a thing which St. Augustine did
not hesitate to do."

What is this order of authority ? Does Erasmus
intend by it to constitute a hierarchy of authorities
among the books of the canon, as if some only
enjoy a sort of second-hand inspiration ? It is not
only the reference to St. Augustine, it is the whole
tenor of this passage which disposes of such an
interpretation as completely foreign to his thought.
What he is saying is that since Christ is the centre
and end of all the books of Scripture, the interest
which we should have in what they say will be so
much more lively, the more clearly the figure of
Christ stands out in them. Likewise, what he says
immediately after this concerning the unhappy
multiplication of dogmatic definitions called forth
by successive heresies has by no means the latitu-
dinarian meaning imagined by some critics. What
Erasmus regrets is that the living unity of Christ
is in danger of being overshadowed by the multi-
plicity of formulae. This, he says, is but the consequence, and so the sign of a lessening of faith.
It is futile to dilate the supposed liberalism of these

statements, for here again Erasmus is only quoting the Fathers, and among them St. Athanasius and St. Basil. [4]

What Erasmus opposes is an accumulation of definitions which do not necessarily constitute an advance or enrichment of understanding since they lead to more and more abstract thinking. He contrasts to it the concrete nature of all the various manifestations of Christ in the Gospels.

Naturally he meets with the objections based on the contradictions in the Scriptures. To these he devotes a whole section with numerous examples, and, avoiding any kind of forced solution, concludes with this observation : " Hujusmodi scrupi si quando inciderint, non opertebit offendi, aut de fide scripti dubitare, sed pensitatis omnibus circumstantiis, explicandae difficultatis rationem quaerere.... Upon meeting with a difficulty of this type, one should not take scandal or begin to doubt the truth of the written word, but having weighed all the circumstances, one should seek a means for explaining the difficulty . . . ''

Following this method, he takes up the question of the humanity and the divinity of the Saviour, and their respective manifestation in both His works and His actions. Here again, the patristic inspiration is obvious. As before, Erasmus follows St. Gregory Nazianzen closely, though not without tightening and clarifying his thought. This is followed by a detailed examination of the arguments used to establish the divinity of Christ ; first those which render the incredulity of the Jews inexcusable, then the manner in which the holiness of Christ has been manifest to all, and finally the way He

---

4) cf. Allen, *op. cit.* vol. III, 844, pp. 330 ff ; also Seebohm (*Everyman* edition : 1938) pp. 272-274.

has drawn the world to Himself.   Following the
Fathers as always, Erasmus carefully establishes
that Christ, for the purpose, made no use of force,
nor even of any of the powers of this world.

But before following him into this second part of
his work, let us, for a moment, return to the first.
Is there now any further need to insist on the ex-
travagance of the suggestion that the Christ of
Erasmus recalls the Christ of Renan ?   What we
find here is nothing other than a very pure outline
of the Christ of the Gospels set in the light of the
patristic tradition.   The only thing to be remarked
is the insistence of Erasmus on these three points :
the transcendence of Christ and of the Gospels
in contrast to the philosophers and philosophies
of antiquity ;   the profound consistancy of the
Bible despite apparent contradictions :   and finally
the solidity of the arguments upon which are founded
the divinity and the messianic character of Christ.
On all these points Erasmus reacts decidedly against
the spirit of a Valla, whose *Adnotationes* he had
himself published.

We cannot insist too strongly that Erasmus,
using the most solid arguments, occupies the first
rank in the battle against the confused thought
that reduces to a common level paganism and
Christianity, against the naturalism reducing the
person of Christ to a merely human level, against the
extremist criticism which dismembers the Sacred
Scriptures without recognizing their transcendent
unity.   The real value of his procedure lies in the
way he turns their own arguments against Valla
and the rest of the humanist sceptics.   His own
scholastic adversaries had been content merely to
condemn these neo-pagans in the name of the very
principles which these latter had been calling into

question. Erasmus, acknowledging the efficacy of the historical criticism which Valla had been the first to put to such good use, now takes this very instrument from the hands of the enemy and uses it to reaffirm traditional truths.

Passing then from the Christ of the Gospels to the primitive Church, and in particular to the Apostles, Erasmus shows how the latter adopted the very methods of the Master. St. Paul made himself all things to all men ; St. Peter was careful not to scandalize the Jews, but to show them how Judaism is fulfilled and surpassed in the Gospel. Then Erasmus returns to the qualities which Christ demands of those who wish to take part in his work ; disinterestedness both as regards relatives and as regards riches, a renunciation of ambition, violence, and pride. Next comes an excellent account of the grace through which good works are performed. Erasmus then comes back to the obligation especially incumbent on the disciple of Christ : never to be ashamed of His Master ; and brings this enumeration to a close by describing the detachment and the evenness of temper which faith brings with it.

Christ Himself gives us the example of all this. What he demands of us in turn can be summed up in two inseparable requirements : faith and charity. At this point occurs the longest and weightiest of the polemical parts of the book. Erasmus opposes this religion of faith and of charity to every religion that consists primarily of external ceremonies. He has no difficulty in demonstrating the contrast between the two in St. Paul. We already sense that this theoretical discussion is inspired by very concrete circumstances ; and these are soon divulged. Those who today are opposed to any theology of the

kind proposed here, Erasmus contends, are those
who profit from a superstitious form of religion,
and see it threatened. But in direct contrast to
their ambitions and covetousness, St. Paul had
preached concord and brotherly love, and the same
could be said of St. John and of St. Peter. This
part ends with an attack at the cost of all formalism
and superstition in Christianity, and with a barely
disguised tilt against the mendicant orders.

Still, it might be said that, whatever its super-
ficial meaning, the whole tone of the passage brings
Erasmus's position close to that of the Protestants.
But this is decidedly not so.

In the first place it is incontestable that he is not
condemning " ceremonies " in general, whatever
he may include under that head, but the attitude
that makes them an end instead of only a means
in the spiritual life. Secondly what he means by
" ceremonies "are not the liturgical rites of the
Church, but the special devotions added to them,
and particularly those which become the monopoly
of particular religious orders. The following paragraph shows this clearly :

> ' What, therefore,' someone may ask, ' do
> you condemn ceremonies ?' Not at all. I
> praise those rites with which in times past
> and today the Church's choral functions are
> performed. They represent something and
> they add majesty to divine worship, though
> in these too there must be moderation. I do
> not approve, though, of having the whole
> life of the Christian overburdened with cere-
> monies introduced by human statutes ; or
> that too much is attributed to them and too
> little to devotion ; that the more simple be
> so occupied with these things that they neglect

> *the pursuit of true religion ; or finally that*
> *because of these things, the tranquility of the*
> *Christian body should be shattered by great*
> *tragedies.*

It is obvious from this that Erasmus goes no
further, as regards essentials, than does St. Paul
in the texts quoted or commented. The only thing
open to discussion is whether his application of
these texts to what he sees going on is made for
good or bad motives. But it is most difficult to
find here any of those examples of extreme hetero-
doxy alleged to be present in these pages or in the
views they summarise. At the most he expresses
himself here and there with too much severity.

There is a third consideration to be made on this
subject, perhaps of greater importance than the
foregoing. What is it that Erasmus really opposes
to the religion of outward forms ? This is the
touch-stone clearly and absolutely distinguishing
him from the Protestants, even the most moderate.
It is not faith alone, nor is it even primarily the
faith which he holds up against mere formal devotion,
but it is faith and charity, or a faith vivified by
charity. This is precisely what the Lutherans rejected passionately in their controversy with the
Catholics, and what the Council of Trent upheld
against them as traditional doctrine. It must be
admitted that no one could ask more than that.

Erasmus concludes this section devoted to the
ideal of the servant based on contemplation of the
Master, with a few final remarks. He contrasts
the severity Christ showed to the Pharisees with
his gentleness towards the lowly. He stresses the
necessity of personal preparation for communicating
the truth, just as he had insisted upon this for
acquiring it. He recalls—and on this he felt strongly

—that Christ used neither force nor guile to win men. Finally, he makes a number of excellent psychological observations on the attitude of Christ to different kinds of hearers.

We shall return to this ideal of the servant of Christ which the Erasmian theology aims at forming. For the moment, let us continue our reading of the *Ratio* to the end. The last part is a series of injunctions, more or less disconnected, addressed to the exegete : difficulties to be surmounted, precautions to be taken, procedures to follow. These make up a body of reflections of great wisdom, whose value can scarcely be exaggerated.

Erasmus begins by discussing the difficulties that are embodied in what he calls the " tropes, allegories, parables." Taking the example of the prodigal son, he analyses most felicitously the effect of the parable in that its truth both touches the heart and instructs the mind. He adds that the same thing can be said concerning the allegories of the Old Testament, and instances Abraham digging wells across the desert, the vestments of Aaron, etc. Following the Alexandrians, he dilates on the mysterious majesty which the biblical teaching derives from expressions at once obscure and luminous.

Next he embarks on a discussion of the similes employed by St. Paul : the body and the head, the building etc. Then he returns to the question of allegorical interpretations. Its legitimacy cannot be questioned, he asserts, for it is undeniable that Christ himself employed this manner of interpretation in his quotations from the Old Testament, and St. Paul as well. But both of them, in so doing, corrected far-fetched interpretations. As a result, they laid down a firm foundation for this type of exegesis, and implicitly indicated criteria, which

Erasmus now attempts to elucidate. Further on, he returns to the importance of allegory properly understood. Without it, many passages in the Old Testament would remain meaningless for us.

Likewise there are passages even in the New Testament which undoubtedly require this kind of interpretation. But it is obvious that here one must be particularly on guard against possible abuses. In the concrete, Erasmus details the reservations to be made regarding interpretations of this kind that derive not from the text itself but from the imagination of the exegete. His remarks apply on occasion to St. Augustine, but are mainly directed to St. Ambrose, of whom he gives several pertinent examples, reinforced by a satirical remark of St. Jerome. In this sphere, Origen seems to have succeeded best : " sedulus magis quam felix Ambrosius.'

This dissertation has a particular interest today, when we have come to see in the patristic allegories much more than the wild fancies they were formerly held to be. It would be difficult to find a modern treatise as balanced and perceptive (on this subject).

In addition to the difficulty arising from the literary forms of the biblical writings, Erasmus indicates various others. He instances idiomatic expressions (in the New Testament the hebraisms are especially misleading), the employment of hyperbole, and of expressions that have to be understood in a wide sense. He points out with great precision what is to be taken ironically, even in certain utterances of Christ. Finally, he insists at length on the need to be aware of double meanings, particularly where a word in the biblical tongue has a different meaning from its classical use. Here Erasmus gives an excellent account of what St. Paul means by the opposition between *caro* and *spiritus*.

Following the discussion of these various problems, Erasmus proffers some advice. Scripture should always be quoted at first hand, with attention to its meaning. This means that the context must always be considered. Nothing, in fact, he says, is more deplorable than the habit of citing passages from the Sacred Scriptures without any regard for their real meaning. This practice is disastrous in dealing with an adversary. There follows a merciless list of distortions found in St. Ambrose, the Venerable Bede, and St. Augustine.

Erasmus then returns to a topic that he had touched upon previously ; the urgency of a work that would set out Scriptural contexts, that is to say, a concordance, not merely verbal but, so to speak, mental, of Scripture. This brings him to a series of rules to be followed for a fruitful comparison of texts with one another. In passing, he indicates and approves the habit of learning passages by heart, provided that at least the literal sense be understood.

Once again he discusses the order to be observed in studying the books of the Bible and gives his opinion on the lines we have already indicated : the student should not wander aimlessly in the Old Testament, but apply himself to the essence of the New. But above all he insists that the texts themselves must be read ; that it is not sufficent to be acquainted with text-books of whatever kind, whether doctrinal summaries, dictionaries or collections of references. Nothing can replace, nothing equal the reading of the text for its own sake, consecutively, instead of merely referring to it. But it can only be read with profit if the following conditions are realised at the outset : " prius cognitis dogmatibus et hac, quae dixi, collatione locorum adhibita—First the doctrine must be under-

stood, and the comparison I have spoken of carried
out." He does not deny that commentaries are
necessary for a more profound study. He recom-
mends Origen, Tertullian, Basil, Gregory Nazianzen,
Athanasius, Cyril, Chrysostom, Jerome, Ambrose,
Hilary, and Augustine. But he again insists that it
is necessary to read them with a definite critical
approach, and to establish among them a certain
hierarchy of values. It is absolutely necessary to
recognize that first consideration belongs to the
Greek Fathers. Besides, it is extremely important
to beware of forgeries : numbers of treatises are
wrongfully ascribed to various patristic writers.

We thus come to the final section of the book.
Erasmus puts an objection to himself, namely, the
method just described will not make for skill in
scholastic disputation. So much the worse for
scholasticism, he replies, if by that is meant the art of
discussing things about which it would be better
to resign oneself to ignorance. Then he gives a
number of examples taken for the most part from
questions then being passionately debated in the
Nominalist schools ; and simply adds a quotation
from St. John Chrysostom, very characteristic of
the patristic spirit, about the mystery in which
God willed to leave the manner of the Incarnation.
Discussions of the sort, he adds, run the risk of having
as their only effect a weakening of faith. However,
he repeats that scholasticism as such is not to be
condemned, but its methods are to be used tem-
porately.

This conclusion immediately raises a more fundamental question. In all this what weight is to be
given to dogmatic theology ? It was soon remarked
that in this *Method of True Theology* there is hardly
any mention of the Trinity, nor is anything said of

the Redemption or of the sacraments. But in such
criticism there is, it must be insisted, a singular
abuse of the argument from silence. It is not required
of a methodological introduction that it should
supply the content of the science for which it is a
preparation. What Erasmus obviously had in mind
in his *Method* was to further a renovation of theology
by the restoration of positive theology, that is, of
the scrutiny of the very sources of the Catholic
faith.   Consequently, even the most scrupulous
orthodoxy has no reason to be surprised that he
consecrates the greater part of his efforts to defining and justifying the discipline he proposes.
Nor can he be denied the right to dwell on those
subjects in which the use of this discipline seems to
him most urgent. We have seen the reasons which
made him place in the forefront of study the figure
of Christ in the New Testament, and the force not
only of his declarations, but, what is of much more
value, of his demonstrations of the divinity and the
messianic character of Jesus Christ.   The same
should be said of his affirmations concerning the
necessity of grace.   He could not, even had he
wished, have continued indefinitely multiplying examples of this kind. But it must be recognised that
his treatment of the dogmatic subjects he entered
on gives no ground for reproach.   Further, his
Method should not be viewed apart from his *Paraphrase of the New Testament* which is its application.
Whoever refers to these must see that Erasmus in
no wise attempted to draw from the New Testament
the a-dogmatic Christianity that has been attributed
to him. He gives their full significance to its most
theological passages, to the prologue of St. John's
Gospel, the second chapter in the Epistle to the
Philippians, the great christological and soteriolo-

gical texts in Colossians and Ephesians. Add to
this that his criticisms of scholasticism has its counterpart in his praise of the patristic theology ; and no
one would say that the Fathers were less strict in
their fidelity to dogma than the schoolmen. Indeed,
Erasmus's favourite authors, the Greek Fathers,
and particularly the Alexandrians and Cappadocians, are precisely the most theological ones.

The fact remains that his own cast of mind certainly did not incline him to the metaphysical problems of theology. Almost the only questions which
really interested him were ethical ones. In addition,
these were the only ones on which he felt himself
really qualified to speak. But it would certainly
be unjust to infer that he did not believe the things
that he did not write about. His ethic itself was
rooted in the two fundamental dogmas of the
divinity of Christ, and of salvation obtained through
the grace of which Christ is the source. Moreover,
one cannot read him at all consecutively without
being impressed by the natural warmth of feeling that
colours all he says about Christ and the Christian life.

No one was less a preacher or a maker of fine
phrases than he, but that makes the profoundly
religious accent of certain of his pages all the more
worthy of remark. We must repeat that Erasmus'
Christianity is that of his teachers, however little he
may have liked them, that of the Brothers of the
Common Life, that of the *Imitation of Christ* in
many respects. This Christianity primarily concerned
for the interior life, but distrustful of a speculative
theology dried up by abstraction, is, with him, made
all the more censorious by reason of his keenly
critical spirit. All the same, his faith in the great
Christian doctrines expressed in a personal attachment to Christ, the Master and Source of the interior

life, remained intact. In fact, this attachment of his to Christ seems to have been intensified by use of historical methods far in advance of his age.

This aspect of his *Method* stands out clearly when seen concurrently with the correspondence exchanged between Erasmus and John Eck in 1518, following the publication of the *Novum Instrumentum*. Eck complains that Erasmus, in his notes, frequently puts aside the harmonizing explanations of St. Augustine, and prefers the exegesis of St. Jerome. He is scandalized at being made to recognize frankly, with the latter, the divergencies between the sacred writers, their material errors and their oversights. Is not this jeopardizing the doctrine of inspiration, and the respect due to the sacred book ? To this objection Erasmus replies unhesitatingly that to try to edify people with pious misconstructions is absurd. Nothing is lost by admitting real difficulties, while everything is to be gained by interpreting the Scriptures, not according to the imaginings of commentators ignorant of the real circumstances of their composition, but following the exact learning of interpreters aware of all the factors that throw light on their true meaning. The fact is, we would insist, that not only in its use of critical methods, but in its realistic application of a sense of history to the thought and the life of primitive Christianity, the *Method* of Erasmus represents, for the first time and in admirable fashion, the use of principles and methods entirely adequate to effect a really fruitful renewal of Catholic faith and theology. At a later date, Maldonatus, Tillemont, Petau, and Thomassin simply adapted to their own use the insight of the *Method*, without always preserving both its breadth of vision and its profundity in the spheres of learning and religion.

We may well regret Erasmus's distaste for all metaphysical speculation, though not forget that its chief cause was the lamentable state in which he found both Scotistic and Nominalistic scholasticism. But we are bound to agree fully with the judgment of an expert as informed and severe as Cardinal Gasquet who in his great work on *The Eve of the Reformation* observes that, wherever Erasmus deals with matters of theology, his orthodoxy both in intention and in fact cannot be seriously disputed.

CHAPTER XIII

THE *COLLOQUIES*

To UNDERSTAND THE religion of Erasmus in its living reality, we must put aside his learned works and take up the little work known as the *Colloquies*. [1] We have pointed out how it seems to have inspired in Erasmus an increasing affection, so that this manual of Latin conversation gradually changed into a series of dialogues of almost philosophical depth. The various phases of his personality are here successively revealed with even greater freedom and naturalness than in his letters.

The interest which these short dialogues retain is, of course, unequal, but each of them, none the less, has its own very personal charm. In their fine passages, of which there are many, they remind us of Fénélon ; with their urbanity and easy grace, they are more virile, however, than Fénélon's and seasoned with a very lively wit, ironical, but not biting.

Their Latin, smooth and elegant, is so lucid and unaffected that it constantly recalls Terence. It is the counterpart of the portrait by Holbein in which he is seen writing with such perfect ease and delicacy that he hardly seems to press the manuscript. A set of scenes lightly drawn recreates for us, in various aspects, the whole religious and intellectual life of the century. Not only the ideas, but the tastes and the atmosphere associated with his personality seem to be brought back. There are at least two of these dialogues of direct interest

1) In citing the *Colloquies*, we follow the edition by Gryphius (Lyons : 1533) which appeared while Erasmus was still alive. For the *Pietas Puerilis*, we used the Le Clerc edition, I. (Leyden : 1703), col. 648 ff.

to us. They are the brief conversation entitled *Pietas puerilis*—and the long colloquy called *Convivium religiosum*.

The *Pietas* is a complete programme of spiritual life for a very young student. Here we see the taste for pedagogy, the instinct of the educator, more particularly of the educational reformer, which was so pronounced in almost all the humanists—in France it is seen in Rabelais and in Montaigne.

I will give almost word for word the opening of the *Pietas puerilis*, which shows the tone and the manner of these short dialogues.

' Well now, where have you just come from ? A game of chance perhaps ?'

' Not at all.'

' From a cabaret, then ?'

' Not for all the world.'

' Then indeed, since guess work is not helping me at all, you tell me yourself.'

' From the chapel of Our Lady.'

' And what were you doing there ?'

' I went there to greet certain people.'

' But who, pray ?'

' Christ and the saints.'

' Ah, but you seem too pious for your age.'

' Say rather that there is no age limit to being pious.'

' Well, as for me, if I wanted to be pious, I would take the habit of a religious.'

' I would certainly do the same, if the robe would keep me as pious as it would keep me warm.'

' There is a proverb that young angels grow to be old devils.'

' I would rather say that it is Satan who has invented this proverb. I think myself that there

is no truly pious old person who has not been
such since his tenderest years. For you do not
understand anything as well as what you
grew accustomed to in childhood.'

' But tell me, what is this piety (*religio*)?'

' It is worship of the divinity and the observance
of his commandments.'

' And what might these be ?'

' They are really too long to enumerate, but
they can be summed up in four points.'

' Which means ?'

' First, to have a true and pure belief in God
and in the Holy Scriptures, and not to be
content with merely fearing God, but to come
to love him from the bottom of your heart
as the Father of all goodness. Secondly, to
take the greatest care to preserve one's innocence,
which means to do no harm to anyone. Thirdly,
to observe charity ; that is to do good to everyone as best one can. And finally, to preserve
one's patience ; that is to put up patiently
with evils to which we must submit if we cannot
remedy them, without becoming irritated, or
rendering evil for evil.'

' Very well, indeed. You are a good preacher.
But do you do these things yourself ?'

' In as far as I can, yes. Every day I examine
my conscience, and if there is anything that
has gone wrong, I correct it ; this particular
thing was not nice ; that word was improper ;
this action was done thoughtlessly ; you should
have kept quiet in this instance ; you might
have omitted that.'

' And when do you find time for such an
examination ?'

' Usually at nightfall, but mostly whenever

the opportunity presents itself.'

' Fine, but tell me, how do you spend your days ?'

The dialogue pursues a minute but lively account of the day as it is lived by a young Christian. He rises, making the sign of the cross, and immediately addresses a brief prayer to Jesus Christ :

' I give Thee thanks for having allowed me a good night, and I pray that this day will likewise prove wholly beneficial, for Thy glory and the salvation of my soul. Thou who art True Light, knowing no darkness, the Eternal Sun vivifying all things, nurturing and enlivening them, deign to enlighten my mind that I may never be tainted with sin, but following Thy direction, I may come to eternal life.'

Then the young man, having greeted his family, goes to school and tries to pass by the church. There he makes a brief meditation on Christ as a boy in the midst of the doctors, and he invokes the aid of his favourite saints along with the Blessed Virgin. Among these are the Apostle St. Paul and the martyrs St. Cyprian, St. Jerome, and St. Agnes. At school too, he starts and ends with a brief thought of Christ. On his return, once more, if he can, he makes another visit in the church.

We can pass over the details for they are the same as are to be met with in the life of any " good young man," as the authors of the pious manuals put it, except that here we find a delicacy of touch and a profundity in regard to the smallest practices which are less usual.

The questioner concludes the account of his programme by saying :

' You are a little saint, doing all these things.'

' No, but you are a little fool to say that,'

says his companion, and goes on to give in
detail the programme for a Sunday or a Holy
Day.

After a more extended examination of conscience,
the youth goes to Church. It is worth while to follow
him and see what he does.

'If I can, I go up fairly near the altar, in order
to be able to hear the priest, particularly for
the Epistle and the Gospel. I try to find something I can think about, and I reflect on it
for a while.'

'But are you not saying your prayers at this
time?' 'Yes, I am praying, but it is more in
thought, than aloud. I take what the priest
is saying and make it the occasion for my
prayer.'

'Tell me more about this. I do not quite
understand what you mean.'

'I will try to explain it to you. Suppose that
in the Epistle it says: "Cast out the old
leaven, that you may be a new leaven, for you
are unleavened." This is how I try to commune
with Christ as a result of these words. Would
that I could truly become unleavened, free
from all ferment of evil. But you, Jesus my
Lord, who alone art pure and without any
admixture of evil, grant that each day I may
cast away, more and more, the old leaven.'

He does the same with the Gospel. And the
youth concludes with an ironical allusion to cel-
ebrants who do not take trouble to read clearly
what ought to be.

'If it happens that the priest is mute, and there
seem to be many who are mute in this fashion
in our country, or in case I cannot get close
enough to the altar, I usually bring along a

book that contains the Epistle and Gospel of the day.'

The Mass continues ; and this is how our young man assists at the Holy Sacrifice :

'I give Jesus Christ thanks for the ineffable charity with which He has deigned to redeem the human race by His death, and I pray that He may not suffer that His most Precious Blood should have been shed for me in vain, but that He will always feed my soul with His Body, and vivify my spirit with His blood, so that little by little, by the practice of virtues in my youth, I may become a worthy member of His Mystical Body, which is the Church. And may I never fall away from this most holy agreement which at the Last Supper, after giving the bread and the chalice, He made with the disciples whom He had chosen, and through them with all those who are initiated into His society through baptism. If I find my attention wandering, I read some Psalms or something other devotional work of a nature to bring it back.'

' Do you have particular Psalms for this purpose ?' ' I have. But I do not so hold myself to them that I would not omit them if I chance upon another thought which will refresh my attention better than the recitation of the Psalms.'

Asked whether he observed the fast, the youth answered that he did not. Saint Jerome, he said, thought it best that a youth should not fast during adolescence. Besides, it is obvious that the life of a student is austere enough. To come back to his devotions, he tries to hear a sermon if there is one. If there is none, or if it is no good, he reads the commentary of St. Jerome or of St. John Chrysostom on the Epistle and Gospel of the day's Mass. As for confession, the youth only goes to sacramental confession the evening before communion, but he gives no idea how often this is ; but as we have already seen and as he repeats, he always examines his conscience daily. There follows an exact account of the conditions of making a good confession ; then the question of the choice of a confessor. The student admits that this is sometimes difficult, since there are all too many at the time, but to the difficulties raised by his declaration: " For myself, I choose a man who is not ignorant, a serious man, and who seems conscientious and discreet," he replies : " My greatest care is not to do anything that I could not confide to him."

" Nothing could be better," says the other, " if you are capable of it."

" Nothing is so difficult, but with the help of Christ, even this becomes easy," He insists upon a firm resolution frequently repeated, on a proper choice of associates, and on the struggle against idleness. Here comes a fine passage on friendship between young people and the conditions for it to be beneficial. Finally comes the choice of a vocation. In considering the priesthood, the religious life, or marriage, the young man above all else must avoid haste, so that there will be no cause to repent the decision once taken. With this in mind he will continue with his intellectual formation, aiming rather at general culture than a too early specialization. The discussion is brought to a close with a quick glance at the different kinds of knowledge. We will cite what he has to say about theology.

' Theology is what I like best, though what puts me off is the way some approach it, and their dull disputes.' 'Many there are who avoid theological studies through fear of weakening Catholic faith, seeing that there is nothing which cannot be called in question.' 'For my part, I believe with absolute faith all that I read in the Holy Scriptures and in the Apostles' Creed, and I do not inquire any further. I leave it to the theologians to discuss the rest, and to define it when they agree. However, whatever is of common usage among Christian people and is not openly in contradiction to the Scriptures I also hold so as not to cause anyone the least scandal.'

It is understandable that Erasmus should appear somewhat indifferent at a period when the mass of Christians, whatever their theological position, were far too heated. His own attitude, however, was the very opposite of that of the Protestants. They rejected everything in Tradition that was not explicitly supported in the Scriptures ; he, on the contrary, desired to keep everything not formally opposed to them. Anyhow, it is by its fruits that the tree should be judged. In this same dialogue, a little earlier, a question is asked about the strictly apostolic origin of auricular confession. The young man, obviously giving the view of Erasmus, says that everyday he makes his confession to Christ. " 'Do you think that this suffices ?' " his interlocutor asks.

'It would be sufficient, if it were sufficient for the authorities of the Church and received custom.' 'But what do you mean by the Church authorities (*proceres Ecclesiae*) ?'

'The pope, the bishops, the priests.'

'And among them, do you count Christ ?'

'Certainly, He is the principal one.'

' And is He the author of this traditional confession (*receptae*) ?'

' He is indeed the author of all good ; but as to whether it is He who has instituted confession, I leave that to the theologians to determine. As for myself, I am only a child and a simple believer (idiotae). The authority of the ancients is enough for me.'

Admittedly there are judges whether Catholic or otherwise, who consider the tone of these declarations not quite orthodox. For the moment, we will just observe that eminent theologians, of the sixteenth century as well as our own, not to mention a number of popes (among them Adrian VI, not exactly accommodating on this matter) have thought them satisfactory. However this may be, we have dwelt at length on this very ordinary dialogue, so that it may seem that Erasmus despite his strong concern for a personal religious life, and one enlightened by a quite irreproachable humanist culture, remained firmly attached to the spirit and the practice of traditional Catholicism.

His *Convivium religiosum* is more original. Here again we give its opening, which immediately creates the atmosphere at once playful and serious that remains throughout.

' I find myself astonished,' says Eusebius, the principal speaker, ' that there are people who find pleasure in smoky cities, at this very time when the country is coming to life again with springtime.'

' But it is not everyone who loves the sight of flowers or meadows, of springs and rivers. Or even if they do appreciate them, there are other things that please them more. As the saying goes, one nail drives out another. So it is with pleasures.'

' You are talking, I suppose, about people such as court attendants or others of a similar type, who think only of money, such perhaps as merchants.'
' Yes, of these, my good friend, but not of them alone : for there are even priests and monks who prefer to dwell in the great towns, for profit's sake, I presume. In this they are not following the practice of the Pythagoreans or the Platonists, but that of the blind beggar who said that he liked nothing more than to be pushed about in a crowd, since business was best in the biggest crowds.'
' This may be a great good for the blind and their advancement ; as for ourselves, we are philosophers.' ' Yes, but Socrates was a philosopher and he preferred the towns to the country, because he was interested in learning, and it was in the towns that he found this possible. In the country, he found plenty of tress and gardens, fountains and streams upon which to feast his eyes. But they could not speak to him ; and as a consequence were incapable of instructing him.'
'Socrates did say something of the sort, supposing one walked in the country all by himself. All the same, to my way of thinking, nature is not mute, and it does speak in many ways, and it does have much to say. It is capable of teaching anyone who observes it, when it chances upon someone who is attentive and docile. Does not the charming aspect of nature in the spring tell us that the wisdom of God the creator is equal to His goodness ? Even Socrates himself in his retreat, taught many things to his friend Phedrus and learned from him in return.'

' Ah, yes. If one could have companions of
that sort, nothing could be more agreeable
than to wander over the grassy meadows.'
' Would you like, then, to try such an experiment ? I have a small piece of land in the
suburbs, not very big, but nicely situated. I
would like you to join me there tomorrow for
dinner.'

Attempts have been made to find a key to this
conversation. It seems that Eusebius speaks for
Froben. In any event, the house seems to be the
one he owned outside of Basel ; and the atmosphere
behind the conversation piece certainly reflects
the kind of sober banquets, idealized to a certain
extent, that he liked to stage there.

The next day the group of friends met at the house
of Eusebius. They are very agreeably surprised to
find at the entrance a mosaic representing St. Peter
instead of Hermes, and right beside the doorway,
a chapel. Above the altar is a picture of Christ
lifting His eyes up to heaven, contemplating the
Father and the Holy Ghost. There is an inscription
in three languages beneath the picture, which the
humanist read with some curiosity. One text
reads, " I am the way, the truth and the life," in
Latin ; a Greek one, " I am the Beginning and the
End (Alpha and Omega)"; and a Hebrew one,
" Come, my sons and listen to me, I will teach you
the fear of the Lord."

Eusebius invites them to answer this salutation
of the Saviour with a brief prayer. Then he takes
them into the garden and under the porches surrounding it. Here the author adds an excellent
description of the place, giving us an idea of the
tastes of the men of the sixteenth century. Their
avidity for knowledge and for moral teaching

turns the villa into a botanical garden in which each of the objects serves as the occasion or pretext for some maxim.

This is interrupted by the entrance of a servant saying that the mistress of the house and the cook are alarmed because the dinner is beginning to burn ; so they all go to the dining-room. Eusebius says a prayer taken from St. John Chrysostom and reminds them that Christ is the first of his guests to be received. The dinner begins with the reading of a passage from the Book of Proverbs by the servant. Then the conversation starts naturally on what has just been read. It is the turn of one of the guests named Theophilus to explain the last verse : " Facere misericordiam et judicium magis placet Domino quam victimae (to do mercy and justice pleaseth the Lord more than victims)."

'This seems to me to be related to the sentence quoted by the Lord from the prophet Osee in chapter six : " Misericordiam volui et non sacrifium et scientiam Dei plus quam holocausta—I have desired mercy rather than sacrifice : and the knowledge of God rather than holocausts." Our Saviour Jesus Christ is the living and practical interpreter of this verse in chapter nine of St. Matthew's Gospel. He comments on the fact that when the publican Levi gave a banquet in his home, inviting many people of his own kind and employment, the Pharisees, puffed up with their legalistic religion, though neglecting the precepts on which the law and the prophets depended, asked the disciples how their Master could possibly associate Himself with a festivity attended by sinners. This was done to turn the disciples away from their Master. For the Jews who desired to be

thought of as particularly holy, abstained from
all contact with this type of person ; and if
by chance they ran into any such, they performed
ablutions upon returning to their homes. Now,
as the disciples were still too poorly instructed
to know what answer to make, the Saviour
responded for Himself and for them : It is
not those who are in health that have need of
a physician, it is those who are sick. Go home
and find out what the words mean, it is mercy
that wins favour with me, and not sacrifice.
I have come to call sinners, not the just.'
Eusebius replies :
' You explain very well, by a comparison of
texts, the essential meaning of the Scriptures,
but what I would like to know is what is meant
by sacrifice and what is meant by mercy. How
can it be that God seems to be opposed to
sacrifices which in so many laws He Himself
commanded should be offered to Him ?'
' How God can be opposed to sacrifice is what
we learn from the first chapter of the prophet
Isaias. Among the precepts laid on the Jews,
there are some which signify holiness rather
than effect it, such as those concerning feast
days, the Sabbaths, fasting and sacrifices.
But there are others which must always be
observed, being good by their very nature, and
not only in so far as they are commanded by
God. God then was displeased with the Jews,
not because they observed the rites of the
law, but because, foolishly puffed up on that
account, they neglected what God desires that
we should do before all else. Full of envy,
pride, rapine, hate, and fraud, not to mention
other vices, they thought that God was

in debt to them because they spent the feast days in the temple, sacrificed victims, abstained from forbidden foods, and fasted from time to time. They took hold of the shadow, but neglected the substance. When He says then : " It is mercy that wins favour with me not sacrifice," I take it to be a Hebraism, that is to say, " Mercy rather than sacrifice," after the interpretation of Solomon in the text, To do mercy and justice pleaseth the Lord more than victims.'

The discussion continues on the typically Erasmian subject of interior religion not supplanting the exterior, but making itself the necessary end of the latter. From there it jumps to another topic equally dear to Erasmus, that of Christian liberty. It is introduced by Eulalius, a third guest. He is at the moment enthusiastic about the Epistles of St. Paul, but he cannot manage to decide on the exact meaning of the words in the first Epistle to the Corinthians, chapter XIX, " Omnia mihi licent, sed non omni expediunt. Omnia mihi licent, sed ego sub nullius redigar potestatem" (I am free to do what I will, yes, but not everything can be done without harm. I am free to do what I will, but I must not abdicate my own liberty). There follows a model of exegesis. The part we will dwell on, occurring between a reference to St. Ambrose and another to Theophylact, is the passage which expresses the whole thought of Erasmus :

'As for me, St. Ambrose's opinion does not displease me. However, if you prefer, more in accordance with the context, as he had indicated earlier, to apply this passage to the regulations on food, in my opinion, when St. Paul says : " But I am not bound by the power of anyone,"

he should be understood as saying : " Although
at times I abstain from food that has been
sacrificed, or those forbidden by the law of
Moses, in order to assist in the salvation of
my neighbour, and for the advancement of
the Gospel, still I keep my spirit free. For I
know it is permitted to make use of any food
whatever in keeping with the requirements of
my body. But false apostles tried to make us
believe that certain kinds of food were impure
in themselves, and that it was not enough to
abstain from them on occasion, but that they
must always be avoided as if they were evil
by nature, and we should abstain from them as
from murder or adultery ".'

This clear statement permits us to perceive the
exact bearing of the idea of Christian liberty that
Erasmus had enunciated in his *Enchiridion*, which
was taken up by Luther in his famous treatise justly
titled *Of Chrisitan Liberty*, and which, in spite of
all, Erasmus never brought himself to abandon.
For him, Christian liberty was a necessary counterpart of interior religion, not, indeed, ruling out
external practices, but using them for this sole end.
This liberty is, as is clearly seen here, the refusal
to attach an absolute value to the performance of
devotional practices. They are adopted either for
one's own moral and religious progress, or else to
avoid giving scandal to others even though one
derives from them no personal profit. But in no
case can sanctity be ascribed to the performance
of a devotional act, or sin contracted by its
omission.

The source of the difficulty and ambiguity can
easily be seen. As long as it is a question of private
devotions there is no problem. But when we come

to the laws of the Church, the question arises : Can one deny to the Church the right in this matter to make decisions which are binding in conscience, independent of any danger of scandal ? Above all the question arises in connection with the sacraments —are they to be denied any objective value, independent of the dispositions of those who receive them ?

The difficulty of estimating correctly Erasmus' position comes from the fact that the same arguments can be used in its attack or its defence. What must be borne in mind chiefly is that he writes as a Christian moralist, or more precisely as a student of the interior life and its special laws. If then he does not treat *ex professo* of the aspects of the problem relative to sacramental theology or canon law, there is no ground for asserting that he rejects them. These things were simply not his concern and so he ignored them.

But what we see at once is what the anti-Catholic Reformers could draw from his writings. They had only to make a general principle out of what was for him simply one point of view among others. The upshot was that, of the sacraments, all that remained was the religious experience they might occasion ; and of the Church's law, merely a law wholly exterior to the conscience, and at times even oppressing it. Against this is the fact that whenever he was pressed on the point, he categorically accepted, indeed stubbornly refused to set aside, the authority of ecclesiastical custom and the prescriptions of canon law. In addition, he asserted on many occasions, as we have already seen in the case of confession, his desire to preserve and not change the traditional sacramental doctrine of the Church, particularly that regarding the Holy Eucharist. But he clearly fought with greater zeal to defend

his own teaching or rather what he held to be St.
Paul's on Christian liberty, even after the specious
use made of it by the Lutherans.

As Cardinal Gasquet saw and pointed out, no
objection to him lies from a strictly theological
viewpoint, but only on the score that circumstances
made the publication of such views inopportune.
Even so, we should not misunderstand his approach
to the problem. Long before the Lutheran Reformation, Erasmus had reached the conclusion that one
of the main evils from which the Church was suffering
was the general prevalence of a superstitious re-
ligiosity that was wholly exterior to and in profound ignorance of the true interior life. On the
other hand, when the heretical Reformation did
break out, he energetically maintained that it would
never have succeeded had it not been able to use
this state of affairs as a pretext. To refuse to remedy
it in order the better to refute the Lutherans, was,
in his opinion, to cut the weed but leave its root.
Hence the risk was being run of merely healing the
Church of a relatively superficial ill while letting
a deeper one become incurable. As with all practical
judgments, this one could lead to endless argument.
Still it is important always to bear in mind that this
is the real basis of what seems most disturbing
in Erasmus from a Catholic point of view.

But let us return to the dialogue. Another participant, Chrysoglottus, asks to be forgiven if he
brings in a profane author to such a Christian
discussion, not on account of any difficulty, but
solely for the pleasure he has found there.

Eusebius immediately intervenes :

'There is really no occasion for calling anything that is of virtue and that promotes good
conduct profane. We must always attribute

the highest authority (*prima auctoritas*) to the
Sacred Scriptures, but not infrequently I come
across something which the ancient pagans—
and even the poets among them — have said
or written which is so pure, so holy, or so divine
that I cannot persuade myself that some good
heavenly influence (*numen aliquod bonum*) did
not move their hearts when they wrote it. Perhaps the spirit of Christ is much more widespread then we imagine. And there may be
many in the assembly of saints whom we do
not account such. To you, my friends, I will
admit what I really think. I cannot read the
De senectute, the *De amicitia*, the *De Officiis*
or the *Tusculan Orations* of Cicero without
kissing the book and venerating a saintly soul
(*pectus*) which has been breathed upon by the
heavenly spirit, On the other hand, when I
read some of our more recent authors, whether
they treat of politics, economics, or morality,
good God ! how they leave me cold in comparison with their predecessors, and in particular
how little they seem to feel what they write.
So it is that I would rather see Scotus and all
his works, along with a number of others like
him, disappear than the books of Cicero or
of Plutarch. It is not that I condemn all that
the former has written. It is only that the latter
make me a better man when I read them,
while the others leave me, I know not why,
indifferent to true virtue and more inclined
to being argumentative. So then, do not be
afraid to let us hear what you have discovered.'
Thereupon Chrysoglottus quotes this fine passage
that is put in the mouth of Cato, at the end of the
De senectute, calling it Cicero's swan song :

M

' " Were any god to give me the power to begin
my life again from the very cradle, old as I
am, I would by no means avail myself of it . . . .
When I leave this life, it is as leaving an inn,
and not a lasting abode, for Nature has provided us with a place to lodge in, not to stay
there. Oh, how glorious will be the day when I
rejoin the company of the souls already gone,
leaving the crowd and the bustle of this life."
Thus spoke Cato. What more could a Christian
have said ? Would to God that the words of
monks, and, indeed, of consecrated virgins,
were always as this speech of an elderly pagan
to young ones . . . '
His friends contend with one another in saying
all that utterances of this sort could suggest
to a Christian.

Nephalius adds :
' This speech of Socrates, in Plato, is equally
fine :   " The human soul is placed in the
body as in a garrison and it cannot leave its
post without the command of the general,
and is not to remain there any longer than it
seems good to him who placed it there." Plato's
idea is better, speaking as he does of a garrison
not of a house. For in a house one may loiter,
but in a garrison you have some duty assigned
by the general. And this seems to be more
in agreement with our sacred writings wherein
the life of a man is sometimes called a service
and at other times a combat.'

Another one answers :
' For me, Cato's words seem to agree with
St. Paul, who, writing to the Corinthians,
speaks of a heavenly mansion which awaits
us after this life : οἰκία and οἰκητήριον, meaning

a home or domicile. As for the body, he calls
it a tent. " For," he says, " we tent-dwellers
go sighing, heavy-hearted".' Nephalius adds :
' This agrees with the words of St. Peter :
" I hold it my duty to keep the memory awake
in you, while I am still in this brief dwelling
place, assured that I must fold my tent before
long." And what does Christ say to us, that
we are to live and watch as if about to die,
but still to apply ourselves to doing good, as
if we were to live forever . . . . When we hear
these words of Cato, *O glorious day*, do we not
seem to hear St. Paul himself crying out :
" *cupio dissolvi et esse cum Christo* " (I desire
to be dissolved and to be with Christ)? '
Then Chrysoglottus continues :
' Happy are those who await death with such
sentiments. And yet in these words of Cato
there seems to be a kind of presumptiousness
that the Christians must certainly avoid. This
is why it seems to me that I have never read
anything in the pagans which can be applied
so well to the true Christian as what Socrates
says to Crito just before drinking the hemlock :
" I do not know whether God approves our
works. No doubt, we have done our best to
please him . . . However, I have good hope
that he will look kindly upon our efforts."
This man then mistrusted what he had done ;
yet, since his aim was to obey the divine will,
he trusted that God in his own goodness was
looking with favour on his attempt to live
aright. . .'
Nephalius concludes :
' These are certainly admirable sentiments for
a man who knew neither Christ nor the saints.

So when I read that kind of thing in such men
I am strongly inclined to say : " Saint Socrates
pray for us." '

And Chrysoglottus adds :   " As for myself, I
do not hestitate to pray often for the souls of Virgil
and Horace . . .' "

Surely, no one could object to these ideas, so
delicately expressed, particularly if he allows for
the enthusiasm of a youthful humanism.   The
passages held to be so shocking, when taken in their
context have nothing to alarm a theologian. Taken
as a whole, they form one of the finest and most
Christian literary legacies of the Renaissance.

We need not spend much time on the rest of the
dialogue.   The earlier part leads by contrast to a
most severe but fundamentally irreproachable criticism of Christians whose life has nothing Christian
about it other than a passive reception of the sacraments, and who die in the same pagan sentiments
in which they lived.   The final section opens with
a word of Eusebius to the servant, telling him to
give what is left over to a poor neighbour. So the
question arises : should one give up his possessions ?
More particularly, if all or part of them, should
they go to religious houses or the poor ?

To the first question, Erasmus gives an answer
which shows him absolutely in favour of reducing
one's wordly possessions to a minimum, provided
meanness be avoided. The second part of the question, however, furnishes the theme for a biting
satire on the monk who thinks himself holy simply
because he is a monk. He points to the scandalous
contradiction between the ideal professed by, for
example, the Carthusians of Pavia and the highly
ornate marble structure provided for them, with their
indifference to the crying distress all around them.

This brings us to another problem which, along with that of Christian liberty, underlies so many passages in the two dialogues. It reveals the second great difficulty which must be faced by those who assert the substantial orthodoxy of the thought of Erasmus, notwithstanding the bold or imprudent form of its expression. It is connected with his idea of Christian liberty, and consists in his absolute condemnation of monasticism, which seems to follow from it.

Here again, however, the problem must be correctly stated. Erasmus never questioned the religious state in itself, nor, generally speaking, what is usually called the way of the evangelical counsels. He did protest vigorously against a type of holiness that was solely a matter of fasting and watching but whenever he speaks of virginity, he keeps to the traditional opinion of the Church. And what is even more pertinent, no suggestion was ever brought against him personally on this score, though at the time even the most heated defenders of the Catholic faith were not over scrupulous in this matter. In general, the life of this secularized monk seems to have been, up to the very end, not only one of unremitting toil freely accepted, but one whose austerity would be thought extremely severe today by priests and even religious whom no one could consider lax.

His criticisms (and heaven knows how virulent they were) bore always not on the principle but on the facts. The question is not whether the monastic state or that of the mendicant religious—his bête noire—is good in itself, but what was the state of the majority of individuals in these categories.

On this point, no more authoritative witness can be found than the *Consilium de emendanda*

Ecclesia produced by the commission of cardinals under Pope Paul III. The situation seemed to them to have so deteriorated that they proposed nothing less—and Carafa was chief among them—than a pure and simple suppression of all existing religious institutes. It was not just a question of secularizing the monks or the friars, but of forbidding them to accept postulants, so that in a generation they would have become extinct. In their place it was proposed that new institutions be created, formed by new men free from contamination by the older ones.

So radical a measure[2] was never ventured, but if we are to understand the structure of the new militant religious bodies created at the time, following on the Congregation of Theatines founded by Carafa, and especially the Jesuits, we must start from the standpoint of the cardinals of Pope Paul III. To them, any reform of the existing religious life seemed either impossible or impractical for a considerable time. This was the main reason why it was thought best to try something new. With this in mind, we are less surprised to find the first Catholic reformers, together with certain of their strongest supporters both in the Curia and the episcopacy, not in the least scandalized by ironies which seem now almost blasphemous.

We may now leave the friends of Eusebius, alias Froben, taking their leave at the conclusion of their conversation, after visiting the art collection of their friend. We, too, with the end of the dialogue, have reached the close of our sketch of the theology of Erasmus, as far as he had one. This theology of his occupies too central a place in the Renaissance

2) We cite here the erudite but confused study of E. Telle, *Erasme et le septième sacrement* (Geneva : 1954). Using the tendentious conclusions of M. Renaudet, this author only succeeds unhappily in amplifying them by a series of impassioned contradictions.

to allow of any particular conclusion distinct from our general ones. Before coming to these, there is one last stage to be considered, the final period of the Catholic Renaissance. It consists of the glorious epoch of the cardinals of Pope Paul III of whom we have just spoken. A layman, Balthasar Castiglione,[3] will furnish us with the details of what already presages a new age.[4]

3) If he became a churchman on the eve of his death, in the sense that he was given a bishopric, he remained the most typical lay thinker who had lived and thought in a Christian manner in the sixteenth century.

4) Again, it must be insisted that we are not following a chronological pattern : it is rather a genealogy of minds than of dates. Pope Paul III was elected in 1534 ; Castiglione had died in 1529. This does not destroy the fact that Paul had prolonged one epoch, and that Castiglione was in advance of another.

BOOK V

THE FINAL STAGE OF HUMANIST CHRISTIANITY

CHAPTER XIV

THE CARDINALS OF POPE PAUL III

WHAT WE HAVE already said about the collaborators of Pope Paul III makes an extended treatment unnecessary. We should, however, at least draw attention to the figures of Contarini, Sadoleto, and Pole, for we find in them the last theologians of the Renaissance properly so called, that is to say the last who belonged to this epoch not merely in time but spiritually.

As to Gaspar Contarini, very little, unfortunately, has been written about him.[1] Born in Venice in 1483, Contarini became celebrated as a philosopher even when a student at Padua. The first and longest part of his life was spent as a layman and a politician. Early in life a member of the Grand Council of Venice, he was present at the Diet of Worms in 1521 as ambassador of the Most Serene Republic to the Emperor Charles V. In 1527, still representing Venice, he took part in the Council of Ferrara, where the coalition against the Emperor was formed at the instigation of France. But in 1528, we find him in Rome as ambassador to the Papal court. He soon distinguished himself by his knowledge, political ability, upright conduct and profound piety. Paul III made him one of his first cardinals in 1535. As bishop of Cividale di Belluno, he was one of the first bishops to reform his clergy and his diocese. Thus, in 1536, after the creation of the group of cardinals, among whom were Pole and Sadoleto as well as Carafa, he came to preside over

1) See F. Dittrich, *Kardinal Contarini*, 1483-1542 (Braunsberg : 1885).

the committee for reform which prepared the *Consilium* we have often referred to. At the same time, as St. Ignatius himself says, it was he who had the incipient congregation, later called the Society of Jesus, approved by the Pope.

But the event by which his name was specially remembered is the conference at Ratisbon in 1541, in which he took part as papal legate. This conference forms the most generous attempt at reconciliation with protestants made by the papacy. This was not, for Contarini, a mere episode of his life. He produced a considerable body of work bearing upon the matter. Its purpose was not to refute Protestant heresies, though it did so most pertinently ; but, like Erasmus, Contarini judged it necessary not to stop there, but to take up into Catholic thought all true Catholic insights present, though imperfectly, in the Lutheran ideas. This makes his work a direct continuation of that of Erasmus.

Unfortunately, his principal work, a treatise *On Justification*, which appeared at a critical time, shows the weakness of the theological structure initiated by the Renaissance. The lack of any real foundation for his personal specualtions and ignorance of traditional opinions open the way to that lame doctrine of double justification which Seripando was to uphold without success at the Council of Trent. But this conscientous production of a solid intelligence, of a man both learned and highly orthodox, only shows finally the poverty of what the Renaissance contributed to the church's theology. What was needed was some noble synthesis, both frankly new and yet profoundly traditional, as was that of St. Thomas in the thirteenth century ; instead we find merely a forced juxtaposition of incompatible ideas.

This applies even more to Sadoleto's *Commentary on the Epistle to the Romans* and what makes it worse, the whole work gives the impression of being hastily written by a humanist turned, for the moment, theologian. An amicable account of it is given in Joly's *Etude sur Sadolet*, published in Paris in 1857. It shows how profoundly disappointing are the works of Sadoleto, as indeed of other writers at the end of the Italian Renaissance. Sadoleto's work is nothing more than an imitation of Cicero, highly accomplished indeed, but just a veneer. The style is *pastiche*, the content mostly a parade of commonplaces. On this account, we are bound to endorse Adrian VI's severe judgment, while, at the same time, acknowledging Sadoleto's high moral character.

Born at Modena in 1477, he early became one of the group of humanists in the papal Curia. He became famous on account of a poem on the discovery of the Laocoon, the merits both of the poem and its subject being somewhat overestimated. Being made bishop of Carpentras in 1517, he insisted on residing there and performed all his duties with a conscientiousness and an amiability that made him liked by all. It was during these tranquil years that he wrote his principal works. Apart from the *Commentary on Romans*, which, to his astonishment, was censured by the Roman authorities, the principal work to be noticed is *De liberis recte instituerdis*, an interesting one though not very original.

In 1550, the same year that Sadoleto wrote it, the papal legate Campeggio sent Charles V a document, famous even now, concerning the repression of the Reformation. In it he recommended quite simply the application to the Lutherans of the same procedures that had been used with such success in Spain against the Moors. Sadoleto himself, from 1536 onwards, not only took an active share in the quite different policy adopted by Pope Paul III but, even more than Contarini, counted on eirenic measures to effect a reconciliation. After being made a cardinal, he took no direct part in the conversations at Ratisbon, but did not give way to discouragement at their failure. On the contrary, he redoubled his efforts to restore personal contact between the two parts, now disunited, of Western Christianity. This is shown by his correspondence with Melanchthon as well as that he even ventured on with John Sturm, the Strasbourg humanist, after the latter had brought out an edition of the *Consilium de errendanda Ecclesia*, which he considered to be a direct avowal of corruption in the Catholic Church. [2]

In 1542, in the temporal sphere, Sadoleto attempted with as little success a reconciliation between Francis I of France and Charles V of Spain. He died in Rome in 1547, where he had returned after this last failure. Doubtless, no one ever held on so long and ardently to the great vision of unity that first rose before the Christian humanism of Nicholas of Cusa. Nor did anyone experience as a result so many disillusionments.

Reginald Pole (1500-1558) is the greatest personality of the group. [3] We have said enough about the cousin of Henry VIII, son of a niece of Edward VI, Blessed Margaret Pole, who died a martyr. Pole himself lived long in danger from assassins in the

2) This publication was to occasion the placing on the Index of this document, a few years later, under Pope Paul IV.

3) There is an excellent life of Pole by Haile, *The Life of Reginald Pole* (London : 1910), and Gairdner's masterful article in the *Dictionary of National Biography*. For the formative years, see Card. Gasquet, *Cardinal Pole and His Early Friends*, (London : 1927).

pay of the " Defender of Faith," and having eluded
this sort of justice nearly became Pope. We
have described the scruple of conscience that had
kept him from accepting the tiara. Although far
more on his guard against the paganism of the
ancients than was Sadoleto, he showed himself
from his student days at Padua in the early sixteenth century to be one of the most complete examples
of the Catholic humanist. The guests at his little
court in Viterbo, such as Vittoria Colonna, the
religious poetess and friend of Michelangelo—the
apocalyptic Michelangelo of the *Last Judgment*—
alarmed the narrow orthodoxy of Carafa. None
the less, in Pole we seem to discern for the last
time fidelity to the Church and traditional beliefs,
openness to the aspirations of religious reform and
the highest culture of the mind, all co-existing
harmoniously in a common fulness of life.

CHAPTER XV

BALTHASAR CASTIGLIONE

THERE IS A small book which presents us with a vivid image of another court in Italy, very similar to that at Vitterbo, except that the atmosphere is frankly lay and no longer clerical. No product of the Italian Renaissance experienced a greater or more international success than the *Cortiggiano* of Balthasar Castiglione. A nobleman, of high artistic and literary gifts, a soldier, a diplomat, and then a prelate when almost *in extremis*, Balthasar Castiglione had been besides in intimate connection with everyone associated with Pope Paul III. His book, from which both Montaigne and Rabelais borrowed freely, was translated and published time and time again all over Europe. It was appreciated in France more than anywhere else ; and by the end of the century, had become as it were the secular breviary of Europe.

It may seem strange for us to introduce a book of this sort at the end of a long series of efforts made in the attempt, over the course of more than a century, to christianize the Renaissance. The reason is that nothing else so clearly summarises the results achieved.

To begin with, in passing from the last group described to Castiglione, we are struck by the ease of the transition from one type of man arrived at the final stage of development, to a quite different type and a new conception of life.

With Sadoleto, Pole or Contarini, we already have the impression that, though the Christian element is still primary, the Renaissance element developed practically independently and the outcome is a distinct culture which tends to become a mere literary virtuosity.

The two exist together harmoniously but they are juxtaposed rather than intimately united.   The composite character of the result is betrayed by the theory of a twofold justification which sticks on to a theology bewitched by the Lutheran supernaturalism, a strongly Pelagian ethic.   These same two elements are to be found in Castiglione, and in the same relationship.   Here, however, it is Christianity that appears in a literary guise, developed along artistic lines rather than as a profound way of life, while an autonomous humanism furnishes the true foundation of character.

All the same, we can still discern one by one, in the works of Castiglione, all the elements of the Catholic Renaissance.   Again, however, not only are they altered, but with the passage of time their original richness has been reduced to a bare outline. Their very impoverishment, however, makes them now malleable, and, suitably moulded as experience demanded, they were to form the material for the more stable synthesis of the classical period.

Balthasar Castiglione's book provided the rising generation with a new model. Yet all it set out to do was to preserve in idealised form the memory of what had already disappeared with its equally ephemeral world. He wrote after the Italian Wars, when the political, artistic, and literary life of the peninsula had been shattered before fertilising that of the other countries of Europe. His preface is poignant in its sadness. Its air of disillusion recalls the last poems of Michelangelo, or his letters to Vittoria Colonna.   The same feeling was shown

N

by all thinking Italians at that period. A civilization
too rich, too intense at the outset, and then too
refined was suddenly seen to be tottering. Its re-
suscitation was despaired of ; men desired at least
to retrieve and to hand on its elegance. It was
this that led Castiglione to recall the conversations at the court of Urbina, held under the presidency
of the Duchess Elizabeth Gonzaga and her friend
the Countess Emilia Pia, between Bembo, Aretino,
Bibbiena, the two Fregosi, and the rest. The subject
was the ideal of the courtier, the companion of a
prince.

The first book gives one last model of a perfect
education, a subject that so engaged the attention
of the fifteenth and sixteenth centuries. It is still
a universal education, not so much in the manner
of Pico della Mirandola but in that of Vittorino
da Feltre, a full development of the faculties of
soul and body. But the dominant note throughout
the book is no longer an avid desire for universal
knowledge and experience. It is rather a concern
for delicacy of taste and perfect balance.

The second book deals with conversation, somewhat excessively for our taste. It is, in fact, an analysis
of the social mentality approved at the time. It
offers innumerable examples of this, in which the
modern reader will be surprised how relative was
the meaning of the word " spirit " or mentality, in
this particular context.

The third part reveals something of considerable
importance ; with the passing of the advantages
of culture from clerical to lay society, women, for
the first time, take a considerable part in it. In
consequence, with their indifference to knowledge
as such, they bring to it their inborn taste for sentiment cultivated for its own sake. The result is a

lowering of the intellectual level, with a refinement of manners and taste. Along with passages offering the most varied and abundant material dealing with feminine interests, we find observations of subtle psychological insight on the necessity of the presence of women and of their delicacy of feeling for what was shortly to be called polite high society.

The fourth book, with its model man of the court—it might be better to say man of the world—takes us far beyond the mere courtier. The perfect companion for a prince is the man who shows himself capable, not only of satisfying his master's desire for a companion worthy of him, but of eliciting his desire to be worthy of such a companion. In this connection there is brought in, somewhat abruptly, though skilfully led up to, an admirable discourse put into the mouth of Bembo.

The theme is Platonic love, as conceived by Ficino, and from here it came to be adopted by the courtiers and writers of France. As Père Festugière has shown, this piece of philosophical lyricism came to effect the substitution of a merely human for a supernatural ideal. By stressing the aspiration to beauty and insisting on its increasing perfection, Castiglione tried to lead from human, but merely human, nobility, which he could so well evoke and define, to Christian perfection.

The harmonisation of the two is made with perfect elegance, but it is more than an adjustment. The ascent from the human to the divine is made as from one stage to another. The contact between these two worlds, henceforth closed in on themselves, each complete in itself, remains purely external. There is no penetration of one by the other. What we have termed humanist Christianity exists no more, no longer is there a Christianity seeking its own renewal in a new culture drawn from its very source. It is replaced by a humanism wholly secular in its basis, and in this way is already modern.

Christianity is still welcomed by it ; but the guest already feels a stranger in the friendly house in whose building and adornment it has had no part.

CONCLUSION

CONCLUSION

WE HOPE WE are justified in thinking that all the preceding studies, however disparate their detail, lead to one single conclusion. In the first of them we attempted to follow the changing attitude of the Catholic authorities to the Renaissance. We watched it pass from encouragement and confident, even enthusiastic adhesion, to anxiety and dismay, then after a first tentative reaction, we noted a magnificent attempt to take it over completely, an attempt soon frustrated by events. Finally, there became inevitable the attitude of definite withdrawal which was that of the counter-reformation, and which Wilfrid Ward characterised as that of " The Church in a state of siege."

It seems to us that our second part, which deals with the interior history of the Renaissance itself, confirms and, in some degree at least, clarifies this first analysis. It should be noted that in this connection we have tried to avoid as far as was possible, any factors that might have interfered with the single aim of our study. By design, we studied the Renaissance in those of its representative men, in each generation, whose attachment to the Catholic religion was persistent and unquestionable. The case of Erasmus being of unique importance, we took considerable pains to establish the sincerity and effectiveness of his attachment to the Church in all his dealings. Since, then, we chose the most favourable circumstances, the lesson of experience, should it be negative, must be given its widest application. Now we cannot deny that this lesson is one of final and profound disappointment, however attractive we may find one or other of the personalities we have encountered.

The general development has been very simple. A real christian civilization, that of the Middle Ages, seems, after the Great Schism, to have been mortally wounded by its own hand. Nevertheless, the vitality of the Christian ferment appears to remain intact even at the most terrible period. All kinds of human values not yet christianized are discovered at the very moment when the existing christian civilization begins to founder. At this juncture a truly prophetic spirit, Nicholas of Cusa, with unshakeable optimism, sketches a plan for a new synthesis in which the Christian faith would reassemble in a wider unity, the newly found riches of a humanity about to be born. But despite his high intellectual qualities, he lacked sufficient command of the material to create anything more than an artificial system, the fruit of reverie rather than reason.

Then with Vittorino da Feltre, we pass to the opposite extreme, to the humbler but more real task of determining the conditions under which the new man could be brought into being by feeding in him the imperishable seed of Christianity with the freshly turned humus of ancient humanity. With Pico della Mirandola we see the renewed Christianity in its enthusiastic youth. Everything attracts him in a limitless world where the same hunger seems to drive him toward both the divine and the human without distinction. All these ideas to some extent conflict with one another and soon everything comes to a state of hopeless confusion. The soul of man weathers the storm only through the power of a religion like Savonarola's, wholly disengaged from the intellect which seems to have almost exhausted itself.

With Erasmus, on the contrary, all is clear and lucid. Each element finds its proper place, but the whole field is greatly narrowed. With metaphysics almost eliminated, with a religious positivism perilously restricted to ethics and psychology, although striving to remain faithful to the great traditional intuitions, and, indeed, capable of infusing them with fresh vigour, Christianity is practically confined to activity on the human level. A pure devotion to the Christ of the Gospel, a precious legacy of the Middle Ages now enlighted by informal criticism, together with a new and profound sense of history, which strengthens the bonds with the traditional Church, keeps within the confines of orthodoxy a religion which some, even at the time, considered to deviate from it. Destitute, however, of a solid theological foundation, because without a competent philosophy, the devotion to Christ, as Saviour and God, seems to float on the surface of thought rather than take root therein. As for Erasmus's sense of the Church and of tradition, it is bound up in his works with what was remote from the minds of his contemporaries, namely a feeling for history in general and for the fundamentally historical reality of Christianity which was one of the achievements of the modern mind that it took longest to realise. To these considerations must be added the imprudence of a mind that was too acute, and also too sensitive, to temper certain criticisms which were adopted and systematized by his most extreme followers such as Hutten or Berquin.

Yet there is a counterpart to all this. If we really want to understand the vitality of the Christian elements of the Renaissance, our study of Erasmian Catholicism must not by any means be confined to him. He was, above all, a writer, and the bounds within

which he confined himself strike us more than his
positive attainments, the greatest of which was the
admirable instrument of christian culture he succeeded in creating. But it is in a friend, who cannot
be separated from him, as recent research is making
more and more plain, that we should look for the
Miles Christianus of the Enchiridon, the student
of the *Ratio*, the youth of the *Pietas puerilis*, and the
master of the house in the *Convivium religiosum*.
This friend of his is a saint and a martyr too, a
martyr to Catholic unity, St. Thomas More. The
limits of this work allow no room for this figure,
the finest in the whole Catholic Renaissance, for
it is that of a man of action rather than a thinker.
But we cannot overlook him altogether. More's
life and death are a most eloquent testimonial to
the vitality of humanist Catholicism, and to the
man most penetrated by the spirit of that Renaissance
of which Erasmus is the chief embodiment. Nevertheless his was but an individual case, not a representative one.

The opportunity for an intellectual and cultural
synthesis had by then been lost. It is true that in
the case of those minds, so gifted, in Pope Paul III's
entourage, we might well say that the synthesis
had been effected; at least they seem to have achieved
a true balance. But its instability was soon mani-
fested. It was a pseudo-synthesis whose parts were
merely juxtaposed. The Christian spirit in these
dedicated Churchmen still retained and embraced
the humanist spirit, but could not penetrate it.
One might even ask whether their very humanism
was not some higher form of decadence. For in
their culture the perfection of form was offset by
the barrenness of content. Little by little it acquired
a content in the society of those laymen depicted

by Balthasar Castiglione as so fully, yet only, human. He himself was not fully aware of its Christian character, which was well brought out by Rabelais and Montaigne. With them, Christianity as a way of life exists no more, even though there still remains a Catholic mode of conduct that is almost wholly exterior. Balthasar Castiglione on the other hand made his human pyramid reach up to its culmination in the divine. But his Christianity, so extremely Platonic in its accessible and illusory sublimity, suggests far more a dream that delights than the faith by which one lives.

What conclusion may be drawn from the whole experiment ?   Must we say that the Christian Renaissance, even considered as far as possible apart from the distorting influence, whether of a frankly pagan humanism or of the Protestant Reformation, failed in its purpose ? It certainly seems so. It helped on the completion and the collapse of one Christian civilization. It was unable to create another.

It is no doubt extremely important to bear in mind that the experiment was far from being conducted in a peaceful atmosphere, as might be wrongly assumed from the nature of our description of it and from the choice this supposes. An immense part of the activity of the Christian humanists was made practically useless for constructive work by the necessity of defending themselves against neo-paganism and a growing Protestantism. But the gravest, the most insidious danger was not that presented by these two enemies but, as the history of Contarini and his followers shows, by what they were able, through unconscious complicity, to foster from within. This reason, however, is not to be over-emphasized; for it is a law of the renewal of civilizations that they emerge all the stronger from conflict and stress.

Should we then conclude that Christianity itself deserves the blame for this failure? After emerging victorious from every previous ordeal, such as its contact with Hellenism in the fourth and fifth centuries, or the rediscovery of Aristotle and his Arabian commentators in the twelfth and thirteenth centuries, was it only in the sixteenth that its peculiar power of assimilation broke down for the first time ? It does not seem that the historian, whatever his personal convictions, has the right to pass such a verdict. What should rather be said is that with the fifteenth and sixteenth centuries we see only the beginning of an experiment of vastly greater proportions than those just mentioned. It is still going on, and probably still far from being finished. Catholic Christianity has by no means exhausted, as the persistent vitality of the Church shows, its potentialities for quietly assimilating the new data which the fifteenth century had first set in opposition to it. If these potentialities have not yet been fully explored, the reason is simple ; it was necessary to wait till the modern order had itself come to maturity. And this has certainly not been attained even in our own day. The discoveries of the fifteenth and sixteenth centuries opened to the human mind so vast a perspective that it is still far from having encompassed it. It is then the future, and not the past, that must provide the final answer to our question. This is to say that the answer does not fall within the competence of the historian ; and that here our task comes to an end.